D0769317

Natalie Jane Woodman
Harry R. Lenna

Counseling with Gay Men and Women

A Guide for Facilitating
Positive Life-Styles

 Jossey-Bass Publishers

San Francisco • Washington • London • 1980

COUNSELING WITH GAY MEN AND WOMEN
A Guide for Facilitating Positive Life-Styles
by Natalie Jane Woodman and Harry R. Lenna

Copyright © 1980 by: Jossey-Bass Inc., Publishers
433 California Street
San Francisco, California 94104

&

Jossey-Bass Limited
28 Banner Street
London EC1Y 8QE

Library of Congress Cataloging in Publication Data

Woodman, Natalie Jane, 1931-
Counseling with gay men and women.

Bibliography: p. 130
Includes index.
1. Homosexuality.   2. Counseling.
I.   Lenna, Harry R., 1936-   joint author.
II.   Title.
RC558.W66   363.8   80-8002
ISBN 0-87589-468-2

Manufactured in the United States of America

FIRST EDITION

Code 8028

The Jossey-Bass
Social and Behavioral Science Series

Preface

---·─❦─·---

Counseling with Gay Men and Women
provides an approach for resolving problems involving intrapersonal
dynamics and social relationships. Among the problems discussed are the
recognition and acceptance of a gay identity, for which specific interventive strategies are given. The general framework for intervention is referred
to as counseling, because intrapsychic personality change that involves
psychoanalytic therapy is not the proper means for resolving the issues
discussed in this book. Our method enables the counselor to recognize the
social realities encountered in living as a gay and to intervene effectively
with a client who is at any stage of coming out to self or is having problems in relating to others. For example, identity conflict may require that
problems concerning perceived homosexual feelings be resolved. However,
this issue may not affect other clients who accept their sexual-affectional
preference but seek help in dealing with interpersonal conflicts or con-

flicts in larger social settings, such as the job and housing markets and the legal system.

We view homosexuality and the gay life-style as viable alternatives to traditional heterosexuality and its life-style; we are neutral regarding the desirability of any sexual-affectional preference. Furthermore, we recognize both the similarities and the differences in the problems, behavior, and attitudes between lesbians and gay men and have chosen examples and problem issues with this realization in mind. We have not included material related to bisexuality, transsexuality, or transvestism.

This book offers a contemporary body of knowledge and specifies its application. Practitioners, educators, and students in any of the helping professions, such as social work, counseling, psychology, the ministry, and psychiatry, will find the book valuable. Although gays make up approximately 10 percent of the client population in social or mental health agencies, most current literature directed toward professionals gives cursory attention to expression of homosexuality as an acceptable and rewarding way of life. Because of this lack of information, service delivery is poor, and gay clients often approach help with antagonism or fear. The information related to skill development here is supported by a philosophical base intended to increase sensitivity by the therapist in applying a humanistic approach so that the client increases self-esteem as a gay person. Because the audience for this book represents various disciplines, we refer to the helping professional, therapist, counselor, and worker interchangeably. Our suggestions for intervention should not be used as a set of recipes. The uniqueness of each counselor, client, gay family or group, and surrounding community will demand variations in interventive styles and procedures. But this book will enable the counselor to move with increased self-awareness, empathy, and skill into problem solving with and on behalf of gay men and women.

Chapter One presents a historical overview of homosexuality, because we believe that the therapist can accept the needs and potentials of gay clients only if he or she has an awareness of past perspectives and recent changes in attitudes. The use of the problem-solving process with gays is presented in Chapter Two, which also includes definitions of terms used in the book. We have used the problem-solving approach with individuals in the early stages of coming out to self (Chapter Three), with groups in the final phase of coming out to self and others (Chapters Four and Five), and with gay couples and families (Chapter Seven).

Chapter Six deals specifically with gay youth because counselors have been hesitant to recognize that some people in this age group see themselves as being gay. The need for social action to safeguard the rights of gays and to ensure provision of relevant services and for the identification, use, and development of community resources are discussed in Chapter Eight. This chapter is particularly valuable to the therapist who is unaware of the network of formal and informal support systems available to gays. A brief annotated bibliography at the end of the book cites additional source material and indicates the theoretical approaches of various authors.

This book could not have been written without the help and knowledge gained from gay clients and our peers, who provided the motivation to write a book that might increase the availability of knowledgeable, caring therapists. These people have also helped us to conceptualize and describe the pain, fear, and joy of being gay. The examples that we use here are based on the experiences of numerous men and women and not of any one individual, nor are they intended to apply to every gay person. However, they do reflect problems for which gays are likely to seek help. We hope that this book will enable clients to receive more effective counseling and greater empathy from counselors than they have in the past.

Tempe, Arizona   NATALIE JANE WOODMAN
June 1980   HARRY R. LENNA

Contents

The Authors

NATALIE JANE WOODMAN is an associate professor at Arizona State University, where she heads the Human Behavior in the Social Environment and Women's Studies Committees in the School of Social Work. Born in Long Island City, New York, in 1931, Woodman earned an A.B. degree in sociology from Washington Square College, New York University, in 1957 and an M.S.S. degree from Smith College School for Social Work in 1959. After teaching at Ball State University for a year, she pursued doctoral studies at the University of Chicago during 1967-68 and then came to Arizona State University in 1969.

Woodman's social work positions have been in family service and child guidance agencies. As a consultant to agencies, she has focused on intervention with women and gay clients and advocation of services for them. Woodman spent 1978-79 in sabbatical research interviewing over 200 gay women in large and small cities throughout the United States.

From that research, she is now developing a study that aims to dispel myths related to lesbianism and indicate ways to foster self-actualization.

HARRY R. LENNA is an assistant professor at the School of Social Work at Arizona State University. Lenna was born in Jamestown, New York, in 1936. He was awarded his A.B. degree in philosophy and classical languages from Niagara University in 1959 and his M.S.W. degree from the State University of New York at Buffalo in 1971. Currently, he is a doctoral candidate in social work at the University of Denver.

Lenna has been involved in a wide variety of social work practice including individual, family, and group counseling, organizational and developmental consultation, and community organization. He is the author of works on interactional teaching, the development of a positive identity for gay life-styles, and competency based social work education. He is now studying social phenomenological implications in social case-work and implications of gay self-identity and life-style.

Counseling with Gay Men and Women

A Guide for Facilitating
Positive Life-Styles

1

Social and Clinical Responses to Homosexuality

American homosexuals have been relatively isolated both as individuals and as a group since the settling of the country. Being exposed as a homosexual or even being suspected of homosexuality has been cause for persecution, legal harassment, loss of family, friends, or jobs. Although this situation resembles that of an oppressed minority, some individuals still question whether gays should be considered either as a minority or as oppressed. Either designation demands special awareness of the social condition of gays.

Many opponents of a more enlightened view of homosexuality prefer to focus on individual problems and to ignore the pervasive, socially conditioned, negative treatment of gays. A review of the history of gays (Katz, 1976) indicates that homosexuals have been mistreated in most of the Judeo-Christian world. Their sexual-affectional behavior has been branded as immoral by religionists, illegal by civil authorities, and sick by the medical establishment.

1

The minority status of gays can be demonstrated by some statistical comparisons. The Kinsey reports (Kinsey and others, 1948, 1953) and subsequent studies (Bell and Weinberg, 1978) indicate that homosexuals constitute approximately 10 percent of the population. This figure is probably very conservative, since many people continue to conceal their homosexuality from professional researchers and most of society. However, even the quoted figure is quite substantial when compared with the figures for acknowledged minorities such as American Indians (3.6 percent of the population in the 1970 census) or blacks (11.1 percent). The aged, who are also considered a minority and whose oppression is well documented (Usdin and Hoffling, 1978; Sze, 1975; Kuhn, 1976), constitute 10 percent of the U.S. population (U.S. Bureau of the Census, 1973). From these figures, gays clearly constitute a statistically significant minority.

If we accept the sociological definition of a minority as being a group that does not have access to the legal and social privileges available to the dominant members of a society, it becomes yet more evident that homosexuals do constitute a minority. The American Civil Liberties Union consistently deals with cases in which communities, employers, and the judicial system have infringed on the basic civil rights of gays. City council actions and referenda that vote down or refuse to consider civil rights legislation for gays are instances of sanctioned oppression. Many gays in small, conservative communities will not risk the social and economic reprisals that might result if they actively tried to change discriminatory legislation.

Threats to employment security for gays continue to arise, as evidenced by Proposition 6, the Briggs initiative, which California voted on in 1978. Although it was defeated, the fact remains that sufficient political strength existed to put such a measure on the ballot. The history of sanctioned discrimination against gays by the Armed Forces and such organizations as the Uniformed Firefighters Association and police forces are well known and documented (Katz, 1976). The oppression of gays by the helping professions seems most outrageous, since these groups are ethically committed to eliminate discrimination. For example, in 1978, one of the authors learned from a colleague that a local social service agency refused to employ social workers who acknowledged being gay. During the same year, we read that a psychologist was afraid of reprisals from professional colleagues if they knew that he was gay ("Removing the Stigma," 1977).

Harassment by the police in various cities exemplifies the denial of fundamental liberties for gays. The right of people to assemble peaceably frequently excludes gay social events or the patronizing of gay bars. In the late 1970s, a group of men leaving a gay bar in a large southwestern city was attacked by several high school students, and one of the men was killed because the police did not respond quickly enough to emergency calls placed during the attack. After being arrested, the youths were released on bond, which was minimal, and though ultimately tried and convicted on a reduced charge, they were released on unsupervised probation. No social activists from the judiciary or helping professions led in the subsequent protest of this injustice.

The Professional Perspective

Historically, helping professionals have generally subjugated gays because of a preconceived bigotry. Until recent years, erotic feelings were considered unacceptable and homosexual behavior was considered inappropriate and a manifestation of an unhealthy personality. In 1968, the American Psychiatric Association declassified "homosexuality per se" as a mental illness, and the diagnosis of homosexuality and therapy for gays began to be seriously reconsidered.

The historical homophobic treatment of gays involved negative moralistic value judgments and prejudice based on myths and stereotypes. Theories about psychosexual development prevailed that were based on biases regarding sexual expression. Judeo-Christian teachings formed the foundation for the negative view of homosexuality. Szasz (1970) points out that what was defined as sin in the moral order became sickness in the evolution of a medical model and that both definitions have equally destructive effects. According to Judeo-Christian morality, hetrosexuality has no acceptable alternative; sexual expression of any other type is a sin and an abomination. Many secular apologists for the oppression of gays continue to refer to questionable theological interpretations of biblical passages. These interpretations now are a matter of considerable controversy among biblical scholars, and this dispute may lead to a more tolerant view of homosexuality.

The religious attitude that homosexual behavior is immoral has had a significant impact upon other areas of thought. Once homosexual behavior had been labeled evil, it was easy to view gays as evil, degenerate persons.

The reasoning seemed to be: If homosexuality was such a terrible vice, then homosexuals must be particularly evil persons. Despite all efforts to locate, suppress, and destroy this evil, gays did not disappear. Conversely, homosexuals also were viewed with fascination and morbid curiosity. This curiosity could not be assuaged, so gays were invested with satanic powers and other myths and stereotypes were invented. For example, the image of the sexual pervert lurking about, ready to molest, recruit, or by some magical power lead others into degradation is still widespread.

The birth and development of psychology could have brought forth more enlightened attitudes. However, religious myths were incorporated into psychological theory, thus giving the myths pseudoscientific sanction. Homosexuality is one of the more notable examples of the medical-psychological profession converting sin into sickness, as shown by early nineteenth-century doctors who labeled homosexual patients with such terms as *invert, degenerate,* and *pervert* (Katz, 1976). Such terminology was employed by psychiatrists and psychologists until the mid 1950s.

In keeping with popular social and religious attitudes, heterosexuality was pronounced to be evidence of a healthy psychosexual development. The anthropological, historical, and sociological realities, if known, were not considered. The pseudoscientific theological belief that the sole function of sexuality was reproduction evolved naturally into the psychological theory that only one ideal state of maturation existed. Therefore, clinical judgment came to hold homosexuality as a manifestation of retarded psychosexual development. Etiological theories about this purported retardation varied widely and gave rise to considerable speculation. Ironically, the etiology of heterosexuality never sparked the same interest. On the basis of untested assumptions, homosexuality became designated as a form of mental illness, and the word entered the psychiatric lexicon of pathologies. As a result, standard therapeutic goals and interventions were applied to cure the assumed pathological needs and compulsions of homosexuality.

Oppression was easily transferred from psychology to civil law just as it had been from religion to psychology. The legislative and judicial systems accepted the theories of the medical-psychological establishment and codified them. What the psychiatric experts saw as abnormal, the law defined as criminal, and it referred offenders to the new secular experts to be cured. The newly legislated role of the psychiatrist as the arbiter of homosexuality was readily accepted.

Individuals who were in conflict about whether they were gay submitted to these "expert" judges either voluntarily or involuntarily and were assured that by doing so, their pathological conditions would be corrected. If prisoners, clients, or patients were bold enough to protest that they were content to be gay, they were viewed as having an impaired psychological condition. Voluntary clients either cooperated with the therapy or were discharged from treatment for not being sufficiently motivated. Having been given the "choice" of treatment or prison, many individuals obviously went along with the charade of accepting psychiatric intervention and finally were discharged. Therapists confidently claimed credit for such cures although articles in medical journals showed other members of the medical establishment to be far less confident (Katz, 1976).

Despite this lack of conviction, however, some results were necessary. To achieve them, the definition of cure was broadened. Patients who would not or could not respond to change therapy were subjected to treatment aimed at extinguishing their homosexual desires. According to the homophobic mentality, asexuality was preferable to homosexuality.

A second response to the lack of success in curing the gay person was to make treatment more severe. A list of the methods employed reads more like a catalog from the Inquisition than from medical journals. These methods included castration, vivisection, lobotomy, electroshock treatment, pharmacologic shock, and hormonal injections. These treatments are not out of some distant past. In the 1950s, one physician considered castration of homosexuals a valid subject of research and another was performing lobotomies (Katz, 1976).

Certainly not all patients were treated so harshly, but the best they could expect was several years in psychoanalysis. Walter C. Alvarez (1974) lists numerous studies that reinforce his advocacy of extended psychoanalysis. This list might seem impressive if the bibliography is ignored— most of the resources were published before 1950. Until about that time, professional descriptions of the homosexual population were based on very small clinical samples.

Despite extreme and lengthy interventive strategies, a significant rate of cure was never achieved. Although changes in orientation might be attributed to a specific treatment, follow-up studies revealed high rates of "recidivism." Nevertheless, the treatment methods and the assumptions about homosexuality were rarely questioned. The particular conditions of the relatively few gay people who became clients were given as examples of the pathological or neurotic character of homosexuals in general. Because the gay community knew of these oppressive attitudes and treatments, helping professionals were regarded as persons to be avoided clinically and socially. Research reports and diagnostic understanding thus lacked even the rudiments of a scientific approach, being based on extremely small, atypical client samples and completely ignoring the much larger, diverse, self-actualizing gay population.

The widespread belief that homosexuals comprised an insignificant number of mentally disturbed individuals was dealt a severe blow in 1948 by Kinsey and his associates (Kinsey and others, 1948), who reported that homosexual activity was not the isolated and compulsive behavior of a few individuals. Among the findings were such data as: more than 60 percent of male respondents engaged in homosexual behavior prior to age sixteen and 30 percent had same sex involvement between ages twenty and twenty-four. These results were so unnerving that the predominant reaction was to discredit them rather than to appreciate their significance and implications concerning gay people.

One of the salutory effects of the research studies carried out by Kinsey, his associates, and their successors at the Institute on Human Sexuality was that sexual behavior in its diverse forms became an accepted subject of academic inquiry. Anthropologists and sociologists began to look at homosexual behavior in various societies and cultures. Of particular significance were the studies of Evelyn Hooker (1957), who found that homosexuals show no greater or lesser an incidence of mental problems than do other populations. Her pioneering work was expanded by other researchers. For example, Hammersmith and Weinberg (1973) found a positive correlation between acceptance of a commitment to a homosexual identity and positive mental health. Data were obtained (Freedman, 1971) that contradicted the existing myths that all homosexuals were mentally ill, depraved, retarded in personality development, or the products of inadequate parenting. As a result of such research, professional help for the troubled gay person was reassessed. The American Psychiatric Association's declassification of homosexuality as a disorder in 1968 was validated. Therapists could not assume that sexual-affectional preference alone was a source or cause of difficulty. The definition of homosexuality as an alternative life-style by the American Psychological Association was another highly significant decision. Almost all professional helping organizations have now taken similar positions. What has been lacking, however, is a body of literature specifically on intervention for the gay client.

The Gay Person's Perspective

Until the 1970s gays had to invest considerable emotional energy in coping and existing with a hostile, destructive social environment. Having their life-styles branded as immoral, criminal, or sick, they constantly had to be on guard lest they be discovered and their reputations be destroyed and their freedom lost. Any effort to express their experience in their own terms was summarily rejected or ignored. Homosexuals felt that mental health professionals considered them unable to define themselves or their experience. Individuals had to be particularly independent to remain untainted by prejudices against homosexuals.

Undoubtedly those gay people who internalized these projected prejudices suffered the most severe effects. Even people who were never seen by helping professionals were affected. This is amply documented by numerous gay writers and sympathetic therapists. To the degree that homosexuals are convinced of and act on the myths and negative views held by society, the beliefs are largely fulfilled. If society for any reason is discomforted by a group of people, it immediately isolates the members and brands them with a stigmatizing label. After this is done, the society can impose social and legal sanctions. When members of the oppressed minority act out the stereotypes that presumably apply to them, the oppressors cite the behavior as justification for further oppression. When some of the victims find no recourse but suicide, it is seen as further proof of mental instability. Others who are in deep conflict and seek relief from helping professionals are used as examples of pathology. These dynamics are fully described in *Blaming the Victim* (Ryan, 1976).

The wonder is that more gay people did not succumb to the destructive attitudes of the dominant society before the 1970s. The resilience that develops among oppressed groups in general was reflected in the gay community. Despite the harsh oppression and the safety in remaining an invisible minority, there was open resistance. Katz (1976) provides an enlightening history which includes protest against the writings of professional colleagues by Havelock Ellis as early as 1897, and the foundings of the Chicago Society for Human Rights in 1924, the Mattachine Society in 1948, and the Daughters of Bilitis in 1955. The formation of gay organizations seems of particular significance. By the 1950s and 1960s, homosexuals were banding together for mutual support and for countering oppressive conditions. Societal efforts to isolate the homosexual began to crumble.

In June 1969, in New York City, an event occurred that was to stir the consciousness of the U.S. gay population and to accelerate its mobilization. Like many incidents that have caused other oppressed minorities to come together, it was not the specific occurrence but rather the reaction to it that had the important impact. In this case, the event was the police rousting of a bar frequented by gays called the "Stonewall." Such harassment of gays occurred frequently—police would arrive, take names, and disperse the group except for a few unfortunate individuals who probably would be arrested on some trumped-up charge. On this particular June night, however, the gays did not accept the police raid docilely; instead they responded with anger and open rioting. What now is known as the Stonewall Resistance marked the beginning of what has become the gay liberation movement. This assertion of identity and the right to civil liberties has kept its momentum, despite some hysterical reactions. Gay people are far less willing to accept the stigma that society wishes to impose on them.

To gays, liberation generally means the demand for equal rights and equal protection under the law. More fundamentally, it means the rights to decide who one is both creatively and socially and to live as the person that one is. Two other aims are also being pursued as part of the liberation effort. First is the recognition of homosexuality as a phenomenon that is not an aberration or an abnormality, as has been shown by anthropological studies that have observed homosexual behavior in widely different human cultures. A second aim is the dismantling or restructuring of discriminatory social institutions. On the individual level, social reorganization means that gays will not remain passive while homophobes define reality in a way that is contrary to the feelings and experiences of gays. Those who behave like Anita Bryant will not be permitted to spread their hatred unchallenged. Gays who feel that they have problems requiring professional help are far less likely to accept a counselor's negative views of homosexuality. Gay therapists such as Miller (1977), Clark (1977), and Riddle and Sang (1979) are providing needed advice to gays about choosing a compatible therapist. Collectively, gays are banding together and forming local and national organizations to fight institutionalized oppression. The contemporary gay perspectives are that homosexual life-styles are not only alternative but also totally positive and legitimate. Being gay is not seen as merely engaging in homosexual behavior but as a gestalt of personal feelings and a network of social relationships in which sexual and affectional preferences play a role.

This comprehensive and positive approach to a gay identity forms the basis for counseling with gays. The gay liberation movement has obviously not eliminated homophobic and heterosexist traditions, and many gays continue to live under oppressive circumstances. The developmental process of acknowledging that one will live a gay life-style may be easier because of greater publicity and increased empathy from the public. However, many gays still seek help because of reality-based fears or continued belief in age-old myths. Other individuals require help in dealing with interactional problems. Counselors who have moved from the biases of the past to contemporary thought are now seeking specifics in treatment, which this book seeks to provide.

2

Basic Concepts, Issues, and Counseling Procedures

This chapter introduces concepts that are important throughout the book. The counselor's attitudes and knowledge base regarding gays are discussed, and basic steps in problem solving are delineated. The stages of coming out are then summarized, and general guidelines in working with gays are given. The chapter concludes by showing how to identify specific problems and how to apply the interventive skills described in the later chapters.

Relevant Concepts and Terminology

Gay is a term that has developed within the homosexual community in the wake of the liberation movement. The origins of the term are unclear, and some people within the movement as well as some homosexuals who keep their identity concealed have ambivalent and even negative feelings about the term. Part of the negative feeling arises because people fear association with the more militant or flamboyant members of the homophile community. *Homosexual* is frequently viewed as a clinical term with negative connotations, and, many gays do not identify with the term easily or comfortably. Many gays feel that the term *homosexual* emphasizes sexuality and excludes other aspects of this orientation. Apparently because use of the term *gay* evolved among members of the gay culture, clients generally find the term more acceptable. However, the counselor should use the term that the client prefers, since the issue is not the label itself but the meanings associated with it. In this book, use of the term *gay* usually refers to both men and women. Where the distinction is relevant, the terms *gay man* and *lesbian* are used.

The positive attitude toward being gay is evident in the definition by Clark (1977, p. 73):

> Gay is a descriptive label we assign to ourselves as a way of reminding ourselves and others that awareness of our sexuality facilitates a capacity rather than creating a restriction. It means that we are capable of fully loving a person of same gender by involving ourselves emotionally, sexually, spiritually and intellectually. It may even imply a frequent or nearly constant preference or attraction for people of the same gender, meaning I (as a Gay man) might notice more men than women on the street or might notice men before women. But the label does not limit us. We who are Gay can still love someone of the other gender. Homosexual and heterosexual when used as nouns are naive and destructive nonsense in the form of labels that limit.

Being gay is not merely the ability and willingness to engage in homosexual behavior. Indeed, being gay is being different, having a distinct identity, frequently in a way that is felt even before it is conscious or sexually expressed. Gayness is a special affinity and a special feeling toward people of the same gender; it is not the inability to love and relate to others, nor is it a denial of the opposite sex. Rather, it is a special capacity and need to love and to express one's love for people of the same gender in all the meanings of the term *love*. A gay life-style, in all its manifestations, is the ability and willingness to live that love.

Gays are increasingly using the term *nongay* rather than *heterosexual,* which has clinical implications and focuses on sexual behavior. Additionally, *nongay* does not perpetuate some of the subtle oppression inherent in the use of the term *straight.* Norton (1976) writes that prisoners originally used the word *straight* to identify those who were not criminal. Gays resent the implication that their life-styles are illegal or otherwise deviant. Scientific writers generally have replaced the terms *primitive, savage,* and *preliterate* with *nonliterate* because of the judgmental and racist implications of the former terms (Chaplin, 1968); similarly, *nongay* cites the absence of a quality without implying bias.

Alternative family life-styles usually refer to those which are other than the traditional monogamous, heterosexual, nuclear unit. Gayness is only one of a variety of alternatives and, in turn, includes varying relationship patterns as does heterosexuality. This book includes examples reflecting the range of possibilities and alerts therapists to the dangers of either replacing old stereotypes with new ones or of focusing on the sexual aspects of gayness. It also is important to note that in describing the gay life-style as alternative, no value judgments are implied. How that life-style is lived, however, is crucial. One of the goals in intervention may be to facilitate interaction for the client that is socially and sexually responsive and responsible. Loving others responsibly with emotional and spiritual involvement also promotes integration of sociocultural values and ethics, personality characteristics, capacities, and goals that ultimately are reflected in behavior that is positive for oneself and others.

As described in the theoretical frameworks of Erikson (1968) and Maslow (1968), optimum development requires that the self be able to mediate between inner needs and a supportive environment. From a trusting or safe and loving milieu, the individual moves toward giving and receiving esteem, becoming autonomous or self-sufficient, and making responsible choices out of concern for self and others. Self-actualization implies that a person is constantly growing and changing. However, therapists usually see people who feel unable to make such choices and who may be experiencing conflict situations.

The client who is attempting to deal with an emerging gay identity must integrate old and new selves, a process in which prior adaptations to one's environment and prior expectations absorbed from other people conflict with self-actualization. The function of therapy here is to help the client eliminate the negative stereotypes that impede self-actualization and move toward a positive identity. The process of developing self-esteem, self-sufficiency, justice, individuality, spontaneity, benevolence, and other self-actualizing dimensions (Goble, 1970) is easier for some gays than for others. The amount of struggle involved in this process is usually related to the degree of oppression or support in the environment. The counselor must be attuned to external factors that create problems and hinder their resolution.

"Coming out" or "coming out of the closet" is gay argot for acknowledging to self, being open about or asserting one's gay identity. Being "in the closet" is to conceal that identity. Among gays, the idea of coming out is more than just asserting a gay identity—it is a process by which an individual moves from the realization of homoerotic feelings to the acceptance of the sexual-affectional preference for people of the same sex. The next crucial step is to integrate those feelings positively into one's total self so that they can be asserted and to find affirmation in interactions with others. To use clients' phraseology, the process involves a "coming out to self" and a "coming out to others."

Coming out to self involves establishing a self-definition. This requires moving from being defensive about one's gayness to feeling positively about it. Such a view of oneself can motivate self-actualizing behavior. Coming out to others is the ability and the willingness to interact as a gay person. It involves giving up a covert, passive defensive social stance in which part of oneself is denied or in which negative attitudes toward gayness are allowed. Coming out to others implies assertive behavior in which the person interacts on the basis of an integrated identity —on the basis of an identified and accepted self.

Homophobia, one of the major obstacles in coming out to self or to others, is the excessive fear of gayness (Freedman, 1976a). It is reflected in the murder of gays, the denial of civil and economic rights for gays, and the avoidance of people who identify themselves as being gay. Therapists can manifest homophobia through their applying old diagnostic terminology or thinking or through their communication about and with gays. Homophobia exists not only in the heterosexual population but also in the homosexual population. Fear of other gays may be manifested in avoiding or depreciating those who are politically active or flamboyant in dress or mannerisms. Negative stereotypes may be attributed to those who have come out to others; the intrapersonal dynamic involved in this situation is related to identification with the aggressor. Dealing with the gay client's own homophobia may be the focus in the initial interviews, and it must usually be faced at some point in the interventive process. More importantly, however, counselors must first examine and assess their own feelings.

Therapeutic Acceptance and Knowledgeable Understanding

The counselor working with gays must accept their sexual-affectional orientation and life-style. This means more than the mere acknowledgement of an alternative way of life. Even worse than just acknowledgement is pity accompanied by an attitude suggesting that such an orientation is less desirable than heterosexuality. Gay clients have no desire to be confronted by therapists who warmly offer to help them make the best of a poor situation. In fact, such an attitude by the therapist is one of the subtler forms of homophobia. Therapists who are unable to accept homosexuality as a positive and potentially creative way of being should recognize this fact and not treat gays, because their fear, anxiety, and ambivalence will inevitably be conveyed to the clients. However, therapists should also be aware of using rationalization and avoidance to justify not providing service to gays or to oppress fellow professionals who do treat gay clients. Haley (1976) has pointed out that once the therapist begins the problem-solving process, he or she becomes a part of the problem for the client. The client should not have to deal with the helping professional's own doubts, reservations, or conflicts. Therefore, whether or not the therapist is gay, he or she should analyze his or her own attitudes before attempting therapeutic interaction with homosexuals.

Acceptance also demands that the therapist be open about his or her sexual-affectional orientation. The gay client is dealing with the relationship of sexual-affectional identity to various aspects of life that pose problems. Regardless of the orientation of the therapist, the client will respond to the therapist's unwillingness to be frank with a great deal of suspicion, open hostility, or withdrawal. In order to be open, the therapist must be secure in his or her own identity and able to convey that security.

Another manifestation of acceptance is comfort in interacting with gay persons. In a sense, this process is circular. If one genuinely accepts different sexual-affectional preferences, one should create a comfortable environment. However, knowledge and understanding also contribute to a comfortable interaction. A strong theoretical base concerning gay identity and the gay life-style is necessary. The annotated bibliography in this book can assist therapists who are unfamiliar with recent literature. Knowledge should be broadly based, coming from autobiographies, novels, sociology, and anthropology as well as from the literature of the helping professions. However, the reader must know the historical context and philosophical stance of an author before accepting the author's interpretations of homosexuality.

Knowledge must also come from experience with the gay lifestyle, including its attitudes, language, and role relationships. Some counselors make a major mistake by approaching their intervention with gays in the same way as with nongays: "They [therapists] attempt to find common denominators as a base for the counseling process. This is the exact process that will alienate the gay client. It is not the sameness but the difference in life-styles with which the gay client is struggling" (Lenna and Rollins, 1979). The heterosexual counselor will find it helpful to seek opportunities to interact with gays outside of a therapeutic context.

Professional involvement is a key to intervention with gays, yet it obviously does not require that the therapist adopt this life-style. The ethnic minority groups rightfully expect that members of other cultures can be knowledgeable, and empathic, and helpful while retaining their own identity. The gay client has similar expectations. Many clients indicate that the therapist's life-style is not a major factor in their choice of a therapist. Rather, their primary concerns are the therapist's acceptance of gays, empathy for their oppression, knowledge or willingness to learn about their life-style, ethics (especially regarding confidentiality), and competence. Even some gay therapists do not meet all of these criteria.

Heterosexual workers can be effective if they are aware of the dynamics that they bring to the counseling setting as well as the dynamics that the client brings. If therapists are straightforward about their motives, limited knowledge, and sensitivities, and if they accept that they may contribute to the client's stress because of their own heterosexuality they will be prepared for the interchange. If they feel a need to defend the oppressive nature of heterosexual society or their own heterosexuality, or if they suppress their lack of knowledge and understanding about gay life, they will greatly hamper the therapeutic interchange. Gay clients will test the heterosexual counselor and become acutely aware of any defensiveness, professional elitism, uncomfortableness, lack of straightforwardness, or heterosexist biases.

Probably the most overriding bias is heterosexism, the internalized belief in the superiority of male-female relationships. Such attitudes are reflected when the therapist (and not the client) sets dating, marriage, and living happily ever after as the goals of treatment. Some gays have reported that after entering treatment with a seemingly accepting therapist, such goals would surface in a few months. Heterosexist bias can also arise in other ways. Without examining the social milieu, prior experiences in committed relationships, or the existing support systems of gay clients, the therapist may push for a commited, monogamous relationship "just like regular married people have." Overt indications of affection, such as hand holding in public or the use of endearing terms, may be discouraged as "irresponsible" or "blatant" behavior because they are seen as a rejection of heterosexuality and therefore as pathological.

Gays themselves have been socialized with a heterosexist bias, and the therapist must be particularly sensitive to the various ramifications of heterosexism. Among these is low self-esteem because of belief in the superiority of heterosexuality. If the client believes in the superiority of others and the inferiority of self, he or she is prone to internalizing negative stereotypes. In summary, both gay and nongay therapists must explore how a gay life-style promotes self-actualization.

Problem Solving

Once the counselor has resolved one's own biases and conflicts related to homosexuality, one can begin problem solving with gays. This approach has general applicability regardless of the specific interventive modalities employed. The authors' experience is that most gays do not seek help for etiological matters, nor do most clients want to become heterosexuals. Therefore, problem solving provides a framework that is readily grasped by the client.

As the first step in treatment, the client and worker together must identify the problem for solution. In this process both agree on what is troublesome in the present and what outcomes are expected. Because problem identification during the initial stages of coming out to self may be especially difficult due to the client's fear of giving up a known life-style, the authors have given particular attention to this situation.

However, to focus only upon such problems will cause those who have accepted their gayness to become angry or frustrated. Some clients never experience conflict over acknowledging their sexual-affectional preference; others may have had considerable conflict in the past but feel no need to complicate current problems with these now resolved issues. For these clients, the presenting problem is *not* gayness but other issues that relate to living a gay life-style, which frequently concern interpersonal and broader social conflicts. While the individual's gay identity is most certainly one part of the total problem situation, the focus is more upon how to assert that identity in a creative, self-fulfilling manner.

Problem assessment requires that the problem-person-situation dimensions described by Siporin (1970) be evaluated. Clients and counselors must examine the social contexts, circumstances, and behavioral or emotional difficulties that precipitated the need for help, including information about prior social relationships, use of support systems, and ways of coping with crisis. From such data one can ascertain what intrapersonal and social system resources are available. These data also help clients and counselors to identify what immediate tasks require and whether other persons or social institutions (family, church) are to be involved. Assessing the problem-person situation also keeps both the client and therapist aware of the social realities that are unique to gays, and it prevents the client from accepting the role of scapegoat for society's problems. Realizing that the confusion or oppression felt by the client has been experienced and resolved by many others gives the client hope in counseling. Finally, because the client is involved in setting the goal, the client's strengths and capacity to grow are validated.

Intervention in problem solving requires that counselors take on various roles. Particular aspects of counseling that are relevant to working with gays are understanding an interactionist approach, knowledge of crisis theory, and understanding the relationship of the goal of self-actualization to the establishment of a gay self-identity. The interactionist approach is a vital aspect of intervention and requires the openness about self previously discussed. While interaction with the therapist is important, it is more important for the client to relate to others as an openly gay person. A gay identity, like any identity, is a social reality—if it is to be valid, it must be acted upon in relation to others. Once an individual acknowledges or suspects a homosexual orientation, it will inevitably become a matter to be acted upon in some way. The kind of action taken depends on the meanings that the person gives to the sense of self as gay.

The client must conceptualize what it means or feels like for him or her to be gay. Exposing the sentiments of the client toward being gay is particularly important since society projects labels and expectations of deviancy. To varying degrees almost all gay persons must deal with the needs of society to invalidate their sexual-affectional identity. Any problem-solving effort must therefore identify the client's sentiments concerning gay identity. Negative, self-destructive sentiments that have been consciously or unconsciously incorporated can be an important aspect of the presenting problem. Even clients who accept their gayness quite forcefully are frequently amazed at the degree to which they have unconsciously incorporated many negative meanings concerning themselves that create relationship problems.

Therefore, a key aspect in the therapeutic effort is sentiment clarification. The authors consider the client's sentiments about the following issues, which have been outlined by Becker (1964):

1.   thought-feelings regarding what has been, is, and can be—the reality aspect
2.   thought-feelings regarding what ought to be—the value aspect
3.   thought-feelings regarding what is wanted—the desire aspect

The counseling process should first emphasize investigating and clarifying these three sentiments, which will govern choices of action. The goal is to establish clear and positive personal sentiments.

Of particular relevance to intervention is knowledge of the stages of crisis and the ability to relate them to presenting problems, especially those concerned with the process of coming out to self and others. The primary goal of therapy, to promote a self-actualizing life-style, relates not only to decreasing discomfort but to increasing a positive self-identity. The development of this book reflects the assumption that while crisis may disrupt coping, it also provides an opportunity for growth. Counseling during the critical period of coming out to self involves identifying the hazards and assessing ways to increase the potential that the client has for self-actualization. Counseling strategies intended to resolve problems in coming out to others, role conflicts, communication problems, or issues related to social institutions will vary according to the needs of the client and the expertise of the therapist. Among the strategies that the authors use are group counseling, role playing, couple and family intervention, use of information and referral services, development of supportive resources, and advocacy of gay rights.

Evaluation is the final step in the problem-solving process. Both client and counselor should be involved in assessing the degree to which the client's goals have been attained. The gay person may still be dealing with other problems, or the client or therapist may anticipate issues that will arise. Finally, evaluation provides the opportunity to assess the coping skills and support systems that have been used during the treatment and that will continue to serve the client in his or her ongoing self-actualization.

Stages of Coming Out

The process of coming out and its attendant stress have usually begun long before the gay person comes to a counselor. Coming out is a life process for every homosexual, and it often starts when a person is quite young and feels the sense of difference that demands a choice of orientation. Coming out usually begins when the person realizes that he or she has erotic feelings toward people of the same sex. A new and often frightening aspect enters into what was previously just a special friendship or a special satisfaction in being with same-sex persons. Homosexual experimentation that may have been part of one's development now takes on added significance. Both body and intellect confirm the desire to express sexual feelings aroused by persons of the same sex.

Thus, the first choices must be made. Yet negative social stereotypes will very likely evoke a defensive effort to ignore these feelings. Questions that are asked of self and brought to therapists include "Should I speak of my special feelings?" and "Should I act upon them? If so, how? With whom?" "If I decide to act upon the feelings, it will become apparent to at least some others that I am gay." "What will this mean to me?" Whatever the answers to these questions are, the process of coming out to self has begun.

In most cases, identity as a gay must eventually be confronted. Again, choices must be made and new questions asked. "Should I conceal my sexuality? Should I go into or remain in the closet?" For many, hiding their homosexuality appears to be the most politically and socially realistic choice. For others, the decision may be to acknowledge their sexuality and to begin to find some social meanings to contexts in which they can interact as gay persons. Some gays can adjust reasonably well to concealing their sexuality, but they pay heavy social and psychological costs. The possibility of discovery and the fear of its consequences are always present. Also, there is a constant need to lie and to pretend to be heterosexual. The stress of these consequences requires continuously being on guard, creating and sustaining an illusion solely to satisfy the needs and expectations of others. For an increasing number of homosexuals, acceptance of the homophobic attitudes of society is seen to be not only unreasonable but also self-destructive. As a result, they choose to find a way to be genuine to self.

Coming out to others demands asking questions about just what the individual wants to assert, such as "How do I want my gay identity to be understood by others?" "What will that identity mean to significant others who are not gay?" and "What are my expectations and desires about the way others should relate to my gayness?" To arrive at satisfactory answers, the gay individual must have a firm sense of self and feel self-esteem as a gay person.

After establishing one's identity, it must be validated through action. This is the process of coming out to others, and it can spawn a new set of anxieties and problems. First and foremost is the old nemesis of the fear of rejection, which may have been one reason for hiding the homosexual orientation. The problem results from the fact that the gay person may have a strong need to be assertive despite possible rejection from some significant others. However, such rejection must be balanced by the rewards of assertion and of finding validation within self and from those who accept the total self.

Being gay will lack reality if it is not validated by opportunities for social interaction. The fact that society remains highly homophobic creates anxieties. The militant position of telling everyone, while theoretically ideal, may in fact occasion unnecessary destructive interaction. When to assert and when to act must be determined on the basis of the potential for survival to be self-actualizing.

General Guidelines

The following questions have been raised by many therapists: "How does the client *really* know he or she is gay? Why isn't it just a stage or one of those 'incidents' that Kinsey's groups came up with?" "Do we simply accept the client's self-designation or other people's label that he or she is gay?" "Would I really be helping someone to go into a self-defeating lifestyle?" "Surely we don't want to have groups for gay kids or adults that would contribute to labeling them!" Before such questions can be answered, counselors must have (1) examined the possibility of homophobia or heterosexism within themselves; (2) acknowledged and conveyed to others, including clients, that homosexuality and heterosexuality are equally acceptable; (3) accepted that the gay life-style has many variations; and (4) recognized that the stages of coming out do not occur in a fixed order and that the resolution of a particular phase does not mean that the client will want or need to move on to another stage. For example, if a client has accepted a gay identity, the therapist cannot assume that this person will be ready to come out to family or employers. The therapist will not question identity and commitment to a gay life-style at length but will be ready to review if and how that commitment is defined and fulfilled by the client. In summary, the counselor will not accept labeling by others or reject the assertion of gay identity, regardless of the age of the client.

The next step will be to move with the client as he or she assesses coping with stages of coming out and evaluating his or her social systems. Social system assessment and intervention also presuppose readiness by the counselor to call in significant others, including any gay partner. Above all, the therapist must not stereotype or generalize from male gay to lesbian or from homosexual to heterosexual experiences. The therapist must recognize the legal, historical, and economic factors that create particular types of oppression for men and women. This caution also applies to the evaluation of literature about gays.

Several factors can be explored when clients hint at or state that they are questioning their sexual-affectional preference. These factors can help to differentiate a person who has had random or isolated same-sex encounters from a person who is gay. One or more incidents or mannerisms do not create a gay identity. However, self-identity should not be absolutely denied or rejected, even when there has been no homosexual experience. The differentiating factors are as follows:

1.   Greater sexual arousal by people of the same sex than by people of the opposite sex, including masturbation fantasies as well as awareness of visual stimuli that a person seeks out.

2.   Preference for initiating and enjoying same-sex experiences. The important factor here is a sense of choice and of commitment and

that interactions are chosen rather than being random or incidental pleasurable occurrences.

3.   Most sexual experiences occurring with same-sex partners. The therapist must be sensitive to the difference between primary sexual-affectional preferences and exclusivity. Although the client may have had either heterosexual or homosexual experiences or both, what is pertinent is the client's principal choice for relationships.

4.   Consistency in number, duration, and intensity of same-sex intimate relationships. Frequently, adolescents and young adults can have strong romantic attachments to people of the same sex such as movie stars, teachers, and counselors. However, assessment involves noting a pattern of same-sex ·attachments that endure over time and that exclude strong opposite-sex attractions.

5.   Expectations and fantasies of the future. Adult intimacy and a meaningful creative life should be assessed with regard to other people who will help in meeting the client's life goals. If the client hopes to obtain help from partners of the same sex, it is a significant indicator of gayness.

6.   Preference for same-sex social interaction. An indication here is the choice of same-gender persons to accompany the client while he or she engages in pleasurable and self-actualizing activities.

7.   Describing self with terms indicating identity as a gay person. This is similar to questions that therapists might ask a client such as "How do you call or identify *yourself?*" Differentiation between self-perception and the acceptance of labeling by others is essential, particularly for children and adolescents.

8.   Level of comfort with heterosexist situations and pressures. For example, jokes about "fags," gays, or "dykes" may arouse intense anger, as may publicity that suggests oppression of homosexuals. Another example is heightened anxiety or discomfort when heterosexual dating in one's social milieu becomes expected.

If the client acknowledges a homosexual preference *qualitatively* as well as *quantitatively* in these eight areas but still demonstrates anxiety or stress, the therapist should be prepared to intervene at any of the points described in subsequent chapters.

In Chapter Three, the basic premises of crisis intervention have been applied to coming out because exploration of the presenting problem usually reveals the fact that prior functioning has been upset and that the source of conflict is in the present rather than the past (Rapaport, 1962). As in any crisis, the professional's role is to help the client to express and manage feelings and use interpersonal and environmental resources. Given the frequent absence of support systems and the oppression of society, working with gays may require helping the client to develop new coping processes. Among these is "healthy paranoia" or a "gay street sense," by which the client can test the attitudes of other people before assuming that they will be supportive. Another of the professional's roles relative to interaction with external supports is that of advocate with relevant social systems, such as family or legal or medical resources.

Therapist as Facilitator and Advocate

As has been stated previously, the authors view a gay identity as a social identity. One does not act upon, assert, or find validation of a sexual-affectional identity fully within the therapeutic context. While initial counseling efforts may focus on the resolution of identity conflicts or the process of developing a positive self-identity, it would be a mistake for the therapist to consider that these outcomes alone are satisfactory. In addition to engaging in individual or family counseling, therapists have a professional responsibility to support the rights of gays and to facilitate development of needed community resources. Advocacy in social change is also a professional responsibility.

For many persons, a gay identity is still unacceptable and therefore continues to be labeled as deviant. This is a harsh fact of life for gay persons, because other people feel fully justified in interfering with their basic human rights. Schur (1971) explains the deviancy-labeling dynamic: "Human behavior is deviant to the extent that it comes to be viewed as involving a personally discreditable departure from a group's normative expectations, and it *elicits* interpersonal or collective reactions to 'isolate,' 'treat,' 'correct,' or 'punish' individuals engaged in such behavior" (p. 24). The issue then is not so much the labeling itself but the *reactions* of the labelers. The social problem is the majority's need to discredit and oppress a feared minority. Although therapeutic assistance may aid gay clients in coping with interpersonal rejection on the individual level, the very large problem remains of collective, institutionalized reactions that impair the gay person's ability and opportunity to live a gay life-style.

First, the therapist must remember that it is extremely important for gay clients to locate and integrate themselves into gay support systems. A formerly isolated client or a client who has interacted in gay contexts in only a marginal manner cannot be presumed able to accomplish this social integration unaided. In larger urban areas, support systems such as gay churches and other gay organizations may already exist. The therapist should know about them and help the gay client to approach suitable community groups. Unfortunately, few such resources exist outside of major urban areas. Those that are available may be far less visible and be very informal. At the very least, the therapist should have gay and lesbian contacts who can help the client to enter a gay social network. Additionally, helping professionals may need to establish such settings as gay rap groups, religious sharing, and couples or parent-child groups.

Mental health professionals must accept the fact that we, as individuals and as professionals, have been very much a part of the problem. In the past we have promoted the deviance labeling that the heterosexual majority uses to support oppressive laws, customs, and social action. The general populace is relatively unaware of policy statements that support gay rights, which have been adopted by such organizations as the American Psychological Association or the National Association of Social Workers. Many people still view gays as sick, bad, or crazy. As experts in mental health we must assert ourselves in society at large and combat the myths and discredited theories that are used to justify the labeling and oppression of gays. Also, gays need professionals as allies in their efforts to change the laws and behavior of society on the national and local levels. The codes of ethics of mental health professions support such social action; passive attitudes such as "It's not my problem" border on unethical conduct. For this reason, the authors have concluded this book with a chapter devoted to the development of gay community resources and advocacy.

3

Resolving Sexual Identity

Some individuals realize that they are gay as young children and have warm, nurturing support systems that allow them to self-actualize throughout life. Many others realize that they are gay later in life, as they gradually become aware that their goals and interests are different from those of their parents, siblings, and friends. Some of these gay people can act on that sexual identity in casual social situations and adopt alternative life goals without conflict. More often, however, these people experience some anxiety because they have internalized societal strictures against homosexuality. Crisis due to coming out to self occurs when the person encounters inner conflict between what he or she feels about self and what has been learned about acceptable social and sexual behavior. Fear and anxiety arise not only from internal stress but also from perception that external support systems are either absent or hostile.

When the clients' own feelings or experiences do not confirm social stigmas, they often question their own reality perception and deny their homosexuality. Such persons may be convinced by homophobic associates that they are schizophrenic or otherwise mentally ill and not explore the possibility of a gay identity. For them, it may feel more acceptable and less painful to believe that they are mentally disturbed and engage in a cure process rather than to acknowledge their homosexual preference and its accompanying negative stereotypes. Other gays may internalize sexist stereotypic male or female role expectations and then experience considerable fear and anxiety as they try to reconcile these dichotomies and myths about homosexual couples with self-perception. While one part of self attempts to emulate a caricature of gay roles, still another part realizes that this is in conflict with gender identity. At the very least, confusion results; at most, depression and alienation may occur. The following are two examples of these phenomena.

Walt was obtaining vocational counseling at the Veterans Administration following his discharge from the army. During the interview, the counselor suggested that Walt would do very well in an activity such as the forestry service. Having recently acknowledged his gayness to self, Walt was confused by his perception of self as being effeminate in contrast to the counselor's view of him as masculine. He felt that he could not discuss this confusion or act on the counselor's recommendations. As his inner conflict continued, he became more immobilized and depressed, finally withdrawing from the counseling program.

Tammy had left what was for her an unworkable marriage and was exploring a gay social group that was involved in behaving in male-female sex role stereotypes. At this point, she was still not sure of her own identity and was told that she "should remember to behave according to the butch handbook." Tammy actually tried to find this unwritten book, but finally realized that the statement meant that she was perceived as masculine "should open car doors for dainty femmes" (although Tammy considered herself equally female), give up cooking and sewing (which gave her creative satisfaction), and assume various other behaviors that would conform with the group's image of her. The confusion and loss of self-esteem that Tammy felt were not balanced by any positive support systems, and she became increasingly depressed.

The balance between available support systems and prevailing oppressive systems is probably the most significant factor in determining the extent of an identity crisis. The sitgmatization of a gay life-style is reflected in well-publicized oppressive attitudes and behaviors that inevitably create some anxiety and fear. To deal with emotional reactions to this situation, the client must actually develop "healthy paranoia," which the therapist should not consider problematic or harmful. Healthy paranoia is the capacity to be sensitive to homophobia. This sensitivity enables a gay to preserve relationships that are necessary for survival or affectional needs. For example, gay teachers in many schools will not discuss their social lives with coworkers because they fear that administrators who find out will fire them. Other gays value their spiritual ties with their churches but realize that if they discuss their sexuality with some clergy they will be excluded from services. Even when nurturing systems outweigh oppressive ones, coming out to self still usually involves a searching process and some anxiety. The time required to find a comfortable, integrated identity may be markedly reduced by supportive resources. Such resources are essential for acceptance of self, and helping professionals have a particular responsibility to maximize their availability.

Meanwhile, for the person in crisis, immediate intervention is essential. Although the phases of crisis will be described sequentially, not all individuals go through each phase. The sequence also does not mean that resolving one phase eliminates all related conflicts and precludes the need to rework similar problems in the future. In each phase, varied coping mechanisms are essential for the clients to retain internal controls so that they can relate to significant social systems. Tearing down these coping processes when the clients have no alternative processes can be devastating rather than helpful. Therefore, the authors suggest some interventive guidelines to facilitate problem solving and growth toward gay identity.

The Denial Phase

During the denial phase, the client may desire or even engage in homosexual behavior, but is unlikely to acknowledge that a homosexual orientation is or could be the core problem for which help is sought. Rather, help may be requested for something not even vaguely related to a gay identity. Presenting problems can involve popularity and acceptance by peers, career choice, dissatisfaction with one's marital situation, anxiety, or depression.

While denying that he or she actually is gay, the client may employ other mechanisms to manage some feelings or behaviors that cannot be denied. In these instances, repression, rationalization, or projection may be in evidence. The client who is using repression as a principal coping mechanism rather than denial may also request help for problems seemingly unrelated to sexual identity, but this client is more likely to acknowledge homosexual dreams and fantasies. However, the anxiety produced by such an admission is so great that the client becomes unable to cope with ideas that are felt to be unacceptable. For example, the client may come to the worker because of sleeplessness and request medication. Although the client recognizes the lack of sleep, he or she is unable to discuss the homosexual dreams. Only after a trusting relationship has been established can the client voice these fears.

Rationalization is yet another coping mechanism. The client finds any number of acceptable reasons for acting on homosexual urges "just this time." Although the client is aware of homosexual attraction or behaviors, there is such accompanying anxiety that emotional defenses are erected. Denial may still be used at times, or the client may abstain from homosexual contacts or sublimate sexual impulses after a sexual encounter. The client may frantically seek support from external systems to prove that the behavior was an isolated event and that the sin can be expiated or the temporary sickness cured. Frequently the systems from which help is sought become partners in the defensive process, and they intensify and prolong dysfunctional ways of dealing with a gay self. In addition to relatives or homophobic helping professionals, the client's homosexual partners during this phase may reinforce the repression, denial, or rationalization. They, too, may need to maintain their defense mechanisms in order to avoid personal crisis. An example of this reinforcement process is that of two women who lived together for five years. Each insisted that their relationship was only platonic and that their sexual behavior was only comforting. They each dated a man at least once a year and denied being lesbians, saying, "Someday, we'll meet the right man." However, at some point, such coping fails, a crisis point is reached, and another solution is necessary.

Following are two examples of the process of the negation of one's sexual identity.

Ann, twenty-five years old and from a fundamentalist Christian background, had been married for five years and separated from her husband for one year. She was in the process of divorcing because she found her marriage intolerable. She was brought to the crisis clinic by her friend Sue, who had become increasingly frightened by Ann's threats of suicide. Ann's own presenting problem was that she did not know how to cope with her three-year-old twins, work as a waitress all day, meet bills, and "survive." The crisis worker intervened appropriately by dealing with reality issues (for example, Ann was eligible for financial assistance and day care) and continued to see Ann for six interviews concerning crisis problems related to the impending divorce. Sue brought Ann to each appointment and finally asked for an appointment for herself.

Sue, age thirty, had worked at the same restaurant with Ann for the past year and had frequently spent the night with Ann to enjoy her companionship and to comfort her. Six months ago, the relationship had become sexual, which was most pleasurable for both. After about three weeks, Ann was "panic stricken" but became less anxious when she told Sue that their behavior "was just an incident." Ann again became very upset later on when Sue wondered aloud whether they were gay. As the sexual contacts continued, and as Ann initiated them more frequently, Sue confronted Ann about their relationship. Ann continued to deny that she could feel or be homosexual, expressed guilt over each "sinful incident," became suicidal, but still insisted that her crisis was only because she needed help with the children and money. Sue felt that she could neither desert Ann nor continue to deny their relationship.

Andy, age twenty-eight, had boasted to his coworkers that he was a "free and swinging James Bond" because he was not marrying but leaving his options open. However, for the past two years, while continuing his high school behavior of occasionally dating different women, he increasingly sought out single men that he had met in gay bars. Repeatedly, after going to their apartments for a drink, Andy would make the "sudden discovery" that these men self-identified as being gay.

Increasingly, sexual relations became part of the evening. At first, Andy denied this fact. When this coping process failed, he stated that his acquaintances started the sexual encounters. Next he rationalized his behavior by saying that the sexual behavior occurred because no women dates were available or because he had had too many drinks. When one partner confronted Andy about the repetitive nature of his gay experiences and activities, Andy became infuriated. He stormed over to his older sister and insisted that she verify that he was as male as the next man and "not a pansy." He obtained her support to seek help to prove that he was not gay.

The example of Ann and Sue reflects a crisis situation because Ann could no longer use denial as her primary coping mechanism and she saw no alternative but suicide. The example of Andy demonstrates the substitution of coping mechanisms as prior mechanisms became incongruent with self-image. At this phase of identity crisis, rationalization may suffice for some individuals when it is supported by associates. However, when a significant other points out an unmistakable pattern, a crisis is precipitated.

Nevertheless, the therapist must be wary of jumping to conclusions based on sexual behavior alone or an isolated incidental relationship. Many young adults enjoy homosexual relationships for a period of time and then choose heterosexual partners for committed relationships that are consonant with their self-identity and life goals. Such individuals, however, may have guilt about their previous homosexual behavior or its repercussions for their mates. For example, the worker may see a client who focuses on guilt and uses projection to express problems, perhaps saying, "How can I stay in this relationship without hurting the other person?" Problem assessment should therefore focus on the pattern of behaviors and the process of forming relationships needed by the client for self-actualization.

As in all aspects of the helping process, regardless of the presenting problem or which coping mechanisms are used, the therapist must create an atmosphere of trust. If the counselor accepts the client as a total person and is sensitive to needs, goals, and affectional options, the client will be able to discuss homosexuality more easily. No matter how the client defines his or her problem, the therapist must identify the sources and perceived causes of oppression as well as the sources of support. Although the client is experiencing panic and anxiety, client and worker can ascertain what coping processes will be effective. For example, withdrawal from sexual activity may work if the client takes on a second job so that more sleep is imperative; sublimation through increased sports activities may suffice; or intellectualization may be used, as the client uses logic to solve the felt problems. Any coping process must have meaning for the client, should be seen as a temporary measure, and should be followed by continued problem solving. Client and counselor can establish immediate, short-term, and long-term goals and identify support systems that will help to fulfill current needs. When immediate problems are resolved, the client and counselor can then evaluate what did and did not work in meeting short-term goals and in reducing anxiety. Then both can assess the next counseling steps.

As the client becomes less anxious and gains some control over life, the counselor may be able to identify contradictions among various behaviors and feelings. The counselor may be able to ask whether the client wants to discuss other feelings or thoughts and thus establish what the cause is of the repeated anxiety or relationship problems. During this process, the counselor may be able to determine with the client the degree to which affectional preferences and supports correlate with indexes of identity as lesbian or gay. The therapist may explore the questions listed in Chapter Two about self-identity as the client provides openings in counseling sessions. Sensitivity to such opportunities is imperative. Examples would include repeated, casual mention of preferring same-sex parties; discussions of dear, same-sex roommates; and wishes that people could understand how some people can feel differently.

The worker must be sensitive to the realistic rejections as well as to the fantasized fears that will result when the denial phase is relinquished. At no point can the prevailing oppression of gays be minimized. Asking, "What is the worst thing that can happen if you are gay?" and then asking, "Is that the very worst?" help to put fears into perspective. Given data concerning supportive and oppressive systems, the client and worker can then explore ways to act as a self-defined gay. For example, when Andy indicated that not having a marriage was the worst result of being gay and yet realized that his behavior is not leading in any way toward marriage, Andy and the worker could proceed. When Ann suddenly indicated that the loss of her mother's approval would upset her most, the worker had a new set of circumstances that were affecting Ann's identity and relationships and could deal with Ann's accepting her own identity and coming out to others.

At this point those coping mechanisms that no longer work can be placed in perspective as the client begins to explore establishing a lifestyle that is comfortable for self. This initial acceptance of the client's own identity may enable the client to believe in the right and the power to choose how to act on that identity. The counselor has created a milieu within which the client can behave according to his or her own values and needs. One example of this was a priest who could recognize and accept his own gay identity, remain celibate, and yet serve a congregation.

The Identity Confusion Phase

At this stage the client suspects being gay but is not sure. The client who is seeking help sees the therapist as a resource for testing a newly acknowledged identity that still is accompanied by conflict. Often, this conflict reflects the antagonism between internalized negative stereotypes and an emerging consciousness of a self that can be actualized in new roles. The client can experience discomfort with these roles as well as fears about losing old relationships. In addition, the client may be anxious about reconciling the known self with the emerging self.

Coping with this process frequently involves the projection of anger onto other gays. For example, indignation may be expressed about gay rights activists and others who are "blatant" about their sexuality. The dynamics are not unlike the scapegoating once expressed toward activists by members of ethnic minority groups. Additionally, the gay person who is still not self-identified may find it easier to observe gays who reflect negative stereotypes than to relate openly to positive role models. Comparison with the stereotypes reinforces self-righteousness and thus makes coming out to self or others unnecessary. For example, the person at this phase may say, "If *that* is homosexual behavior, then obviously I'm not really gay."

Anger may also be projected onto the counselor. If the client considers homosexuality negative while the therapist is open to it, the therapist may be viewed negatively. The gay person may also have reality-based anger toward those systems that perpetuate homophobia and heterosexism. The client may be quite familiar with the history of oppression by the helping professions but be seeking help as a last resort. Despite the therapist's acceptance, the client must be able to express anger without the therapist becoming defensive.

Repression of self-identity or the projection of unacceptable aspects of self may be manifested during problem assessment. Part of one's total identity is awareness of one's sexuality and how one can give and receive pleasure. Self-denigration by the gay client may be projected into various sexual practices, or the client may repress desires for such practices. Examples may be confining oneself to kissing and cuddling and avoiding cunnilingus or anal intercourse. Alternatively, the counselor may encounter reaction formation, which can be seen as an extension of projection. For example, a gay woman might indulge in ultrafeminine behavior and make vehement attacks on gays within her church group while maintaining a homosexual relationship with her married friend. In such instances, the client still cannot accept a positive self-identity as a gay person.

Anger may be coped with by overidentifying with the negative responses of others. By acting on this internalized negative self-image, the client seeks to be punished or condemned and simultaneously seeks to punish those viewed as oppressors. The client almost seems to be issuing a challenge to the therapist or significant others: "So what are you going to do about it?" Here the therapist must recognize that the client does not see the goodness of both the old and new selves. This inability to integrate self-identity is frequently reinforced by oppressive systems or by the absence of support systems.

Bill, a thirty-two-year-old lawyer, came to a therapist whom he located by an anonymous phone call to the local gay coalition. He indicated that he was having trouble with his marriage because he was spending increasing amounts of time away from his wife and children. He had found himself frequently leaving the house after a meaningless quarrel and then wandering in an area of town that had a few gay bars. Every time, he would go into one of these bars because he said he was thirsty. There he noticed "all those men who obviously had dyed their hair, wore elaborate jewelry, or were 'into leather.' " He frequently picked up some of these men for casual sexual encounters but insisted that he was not gay because he still dressed and behaved like a lawyer and was married. When questioned about the possibility of talking with other men in the gay coalition or with men in the bars other than those he perceived as being very different from himself, Bill insisted that everyone who was gay was stereotypical.

Barbara, age twenty-three, was referred to a medical social worker because of ulcerative colitis, which had erupted when her engagement to Mark ended. Two months after treatment, she and her female roommate of eight months moved from being close companions into an intense sexual-emotional relationship. Within two weeks, Barbara cut her shoulder-length red hair into a "Clark Gable" look, bought a new wardrobe that included a tailored man's suit and men's shirts, assumed a "stomping" gait in gay relationships, and came to interviews with her new identity.

Simultaneously, she wore long-haired wigs and frilly dresses to visit her parents and to go to her job. She described herself as being "positively schizophrenic" and having no identity. She constantly berated herself for her secret identity, and her colitis flared up and almost required hospitalization.

Bill sees only stereotypes that prevent him from addressing his own sexual interests and behavior, and refuses to join groups that might validate his newly felt identity. Barbara reflects the ambivalence related to the "Am I? If so, who am I?" questions. Even the literature sought during this phase frequently confirms heterosexist stereotypes.

The primary foci of intervention during the identity confusion phase are the client's own self-image, identification of potential gay support systems, and redirecting anger toward felt and real oppression. Also, a known life-style must be reconciled with a new self-identity for which there has been no prior socialization. The counselor should help the client to focus on self and perceptions related to what one has been, what one is now, and how one wishes to be. Growth of positive self-identity may be facilitated by asking questions such as "How do you really identify yourself?" Even changes in the name one goes by can provide openings for self-other identification. For example, shifts from Bill Junior to Billy Joe or from Henrietta to Hank enable the client to explore self-image and how one actualizes this with others. Discovering personal attributes that the client values can also be helpful. For example, the therapist can ask the following questions "What qualities make you "you?" "What qualities are part of loving someone of any sex?" "What qualities are part of loving someone of the same sex?" "Do you feel that these attributes are part of a self you could like?" The therapist may be able to help the client list others who are gay and who are admired as self-actualizing people. The client should then be helped to identify qualities in self that are similar to the qualities of those people who are respected.

Questioning related to anger that has been projected onto others enables the client to resolve some of the fears and resentments arising from contradictions in self-identity and stereotypes. At this juncture the worker can begin to explore the stereotypes and show the client the infinite variety of behaviors and personalities within the gay culture. To do this, the worker must have accurate knowledge about the gay community and not be limited to information gleaned from myths, novels, films, and professional literature that describe a life of gloom and unhappiness. Similarly, identifying meaningful role models, showing recent writings that support a positive gay self-image, and referring the client to social and therapeutic resources that include responsible members of the homophile community may be useful.

Another way to improve a negative self-image is to help the client direct anger toward homophobic groups. Sensitizing the client to gay jokes and caricatures can help direct his or her anger toward appropriate others rather than blaming the victims with whom the client has an affinity. As this anger becomes redirected, the counselor must let it be expressed within the therapeutic context. Above all, such feelings should not be ignored, this reality-based anger must be validated. Awareness of the subtleties of identification with the oppressor is also necessary. Some clients may report "funny" incidents of colleagues referring to gay co-workers derogatorily or repeat gay jokes in order to deal with their painful sensitivity to oppression and their lack of conviction that it is better to be righteously angry. The worker should not only hear but also question the underlying pain and anger.

In asking, "What is there to be angry about if you self-identify as gay?", the worker must be prepared to deal with the fears of disclosure to others and be supportive of the client's feeling of shock if any of his or her associates find out that the client is gay. If the client is encouraged to vent anger at oppressive systems too strongly, he or she may return to the denial stage ("If being gay means I have to do that, then you've just proved that I'm not gay") or become uncharacteristically hostile and aggressive. The use of supportive groups with whom to share anger and to be open may also be useful. Occasionally the recently self-acknowledged gay finds that boycotting stores, products, or community activities that are associated with homophobia is an appropriate way to vent anger.

Finally, for the client who identifies being gay with negative stereotypes, the therapist should explore the degree to which these stereotypes apply to the client. Questions can be asked such as the following: "Do you feel you are really behaving this way or are you acting a part to show parents or straights in general?" "What do you want for yourself, and how can you best meet your goals?" "Who says that this is the right way for you to behave?" During this process, the counselor can accept the need of the client to test stereotypes and give permission to do so. However, the client must be aware of potential hazards such as losing a job because of violating employment procedures or being expected to engage in sadomasochism because of his or her choice of clothing, which may have certain meanings among some gays. Also, the counselor may find that

the client identifies with a clique that has unwritten rules about role
dichotomies—the queen-butch, butch-femme stereotypes, for example—
because the clique lacks other reference groups. Helping a client to use
alternative resources may broaden his or her perspectives and increase
the potential for self-actualizing.

What is crucial throughout this phase is that the client realize
what behaviors are consonant with self-identity; direct anger toward
oppressors and not project, internalize, or randomly act on his or her
anger; and begin to view gay culture positively.

The Bargaining Phase

At this phase, the client may accept that he or she is gay but want
to become heterosexual. The client feels overwhelmed by the implications
of gayness and unable to cope with the growth process required. At this
point feelings of relief, joy, and self-affirmation alternate with feelings of
guilt. If the person cannot cope with his or her attractions and being
identified as gay, even self-identified, the client will seek help.

At this point the client has both a desire to revert to his or her
previous life-style and an awareness that old coping mechansims don't
work. As the conflict increases, the client is further plagued by remaining
negative self-images, which bring about shame and guilt. Coping with these
feelings may involve putting some feelings and behaviors into a compart-
ment in life labeled gay while others are seen as part of still being straight.
Other ways of coping include avoiding and withdrawing from all gay associations. For example, appeals for help are frequently accompanied by
promises of "better" behavior if the client is "reformed." Such promises
include "I'll only be a homosexual in gay bars on Saturdays" and "Yes,
I will marry Jane in a great big wedding to please my parents."

The counselor at this phase is perceived as an extension of God,
an external superego, or a magical agent of change. The client expects that
the counselor can make reality disappear. The basic dynamics are failure
to be responsible for self and an appeal to external control. As in prior
phases, these dynamics may be reinforced by significant others. Parents,
spouses, and friends may not only encourage appeals to higher authorities
but also actively intervene in the referral and treatment process.

Chuck, age thirty, came to the family service worker with his
fiancee, Mary, for premarital counseling. Chuck acknowledged to him-

self, Mary, and the worker that he had had a homosexual relationship with John for the past six months and that he had had numerous gay contacts since adolescence. He had thought for a number of years that this was "just normal teenage experimentation." However, during the months with John, "everything seemed too right and peaceful." When Chuck talked with his minister about the relationship, he once again became aware of the "sinfulness" of his behavior and decided that he had to do something. He turned to his good friend Mary, who agreed that he just needed to marry her and he would be "saved." She did feel, however, that they should seek counseling to insure that they would have a satisfactory sexual adjustment. Chuck and Mary wanted the social worker to eliminate Chuck's homosexual urges.

Twenty-year-old Carol, after two years in a relationship with Flo, had talked with her mother, who considered Carol as "a friend and a daughter," about her relationship. Her mother was shocked and told her that she had a "very serious sickness" that needed help. Her mother then called the mental health center and came along with Carol so that they both could find out "what had gone wrong in Carol's childhood" and what the mother could do "to make Carol better." The mother had heard that psychoanalysis and behavioral conditioning could cure such behavior, and stated that she would do anything to help Carol rid herself of this "terrible thing."

During intervention for clients in the bargaining phase, the worker must be particularly aware of tendencies to take over the client's problem or life. Tripp (1975) states that there is little or no basis to hope for a "cure." Explaining that one is not capable of sudden change may frighten clients who are seeking external control unless the worker also tells the clients that he or she believes in their ability to choose their own behaviors. Clients may also become angry when told that no cure is possible and displace anger onto the therapist. Although the counselor may make his or her own capacities and role clear, clients may need to test the consistency of the worker or seek other authorities. This choice must also be respected. The client should not be made to feel guilty for trying other options or for leaving treatment for a while and then returning. The therapist should not exacerbate the guilt that causes this frantic search.

However, if the helping professional adopts a nondefensive stance, the client may be enabled to refocus the anger by exploring its real sources.

The process begins by redirecting anger from the therapist or the world at large to those people who have controlled the client in the past or who now seek control. The next step is to identify the oppressive systems that perpetuate negative stereotypes. Client and worker then can work together to focus on the client's expectations of authority figures and the degree to which they actually wield power. Such reality testing can help the client to identify what goals and behaviors are congruent with his or her cultural and ethical values and to locate support systems that will validate a gay life-style. This step provides supportive controls that reduce anxiety immediately.

During the next interviews, the client can take more responsibility for self and the meaning of a gay identity. Here, as in previous phases, the worker will probably encounter internalized negative stereotypes. Questioning what is so bad about being gay enables the client to examine the realities of living a gay life rather than accepting misconceptions. During this process, the client must take responsibility for his or her choices. Two significant choices involve how to integrate a gay identity and what behaviors reflect that identity. In order to attain integrity, the client must examine things that are valued humanistically in the light of self-identified gayness. For example, if close relationships with family members are valued but the family cannot accept homosexuality, the client must reconcile his or her behaviors in the two different contexts. Questions the client should ask include: "Can I be a total loving person in my gay relationships and then be a total loving person with my family?" "Can I relate to family without mentioning the part of my life that would damage the relationships that I cherish?"

In another example, the client may value his or her religion, which may consider homosexuality sinful. Intervention would make the client examine those religious values that are meaningful. Questions here would include: "Can I reflect my own loving of God and caring for others as a gay within my religion?" "Can I believe that my religion is right for me and right with God even if others within my church do not agree?" The therapist can refer the client to gay-oriented denominational and nondenominational groups that will help the client make decisions. For example, the worker should be aware of Dignity within Catholicism, Integrity within Episcopalianism, and the ecumenical church services at Metropolitan Community Churches. Many other denominations have groups and publish material that provide theological support for a homosexual life-style. Neither client nor worker should view these resources as final authorities; rather they should be considered supports for the client's own values and choices. The counselor's role during this exploration process must continue to be that of enabling the client to evaluate and choose. The client must retain responsibility for decisions that can be comfortably made in the context of a total self-identity.

Another dimension of integrating old and new identities requires that the client identify those strengths that have helped to create a positive self-image in the past. The client should realize that these assets remain and can be used in new ways that are fulfilling for self and others. For example, the successful teacher can identify those nurturing qualities that have made for positive student experiences and continue to use them in current relationships with students despite fears about accepting a gay identity. In the process of identifying strengths, the client must take responsibility for defining a good self. Client and counselor may then discard the shame ascribed by others and reexamine internalized guilt feelings so that the client can develop new self-esteem.

The Depression Phase

Depression may arise in clients who have not found workable coping mechanisms or who have not moved from the phases described above to acceptance of a gay identity. The feeling may be characterized as: "My repressions haven't worked; my projection hasn't worked; I tried to bargain with greater forces and that didn't work. All of these defenses have fallen apart. God, neither you nor anyone else can help." No external controls or supports seem available, and the self is seen as inadequate to deal with the identity crisis. The client at this phase is well aware of a gay identity, so denial is not a primary coping mechanism. Also, rather than projecting anger onto others or attempting to rely on external controls, the client can only direct feelings of guilt into self. The inability to deal with gayness may be reflected in such presenting problems as a sense of powerlessness regarding life in general, suicidal impulses, drug abuse and alcoholism, withdrawal from gay and nongay friends and associates, acute feelings of a "loss of self," and frenetic activity to mask depression.

The worker must first differentiate between chronic or neurotic depression and situational depression. Long-standing depression or physiological problems are not the basic difficulty. Situational depression is related to the loss of former self and of adaptive coping patterns. It is coupled with a lack of meaningful internal or external supports. Helping the client to identify the incident or incidents that precipitated the presenting problem can help in assessing the problem. If the depression is related to an identity crisis, then the intervention described here is appropriate. However, if there are indications of a physiological origin, chronic anxiety, or severe or prolonged stress, the worker's intervention would proceed differently (Cammer, 1969).

A major problem for the gay client is the loss of self-esteem due to the loss or absence of family, friend, or group supports that could help in reconciling self-identity with negative stereotypes, dealing with oppressive systems, or dealing with loneliness and isolation. However, there is indeed a sense of self as a reality still worth saving. Once more, the client and worker are concerned with internalized negative stereotypes, guilt, and anger at those oppressive systems that perpetuate the stereotypes.

Doris was referred to the women's alcohol counselor after having been arrested for drunken driving. As a recently graduated psychologist, she was very concerned about the effects that this offense would have on her employer if it were revealed. Doris muttered that she probably shouldn't care about what happened but that she knew that she was "damn good" in her work with emotionally disturbed children and could not abandon them. She usually did not drink very much, but she revealed after questioning that she had just realized before graduation that she was lesbian and that she then felt her whole world slip away. She did not know where she could go to talk without seeing professional colleagues who might ruin her new career. After three months of isolation, she finally went to a gay bar in a distant city. She felt even more isolated and reverted to drinking by herself.

Don requested an appointment at the mental health center because he felt helpless about where he was going. He was a successful computer programmer who had just requested a job transfer to get away from friends and relatives. He now felt that he was "in the wrong job, the wrong place, the wrong life." He had been working ten hours a day, six days a week. He was up at six every morning to go to mass, went out to local bars until one o'clock (ascertained by the worker to be gay bars), had seen two doctors for sleeping pills, but still could not get peace of mind.

During this phase of problem solving, active outreach to the client is essential. The client may be unable to do more than indicate pain and a need for help. Therefore, the therapist may have to initiate activity by setting definite appointment times and being flexible about these times so that the client can meet with the worker. The worker may even make some home visits if transportation is a problem. Finally, the counselor may need to be assertive and say, "I want to see and talk with you." In conjunction with psychiatric and medical consultation, the client may need antidepressants to resume regular activity while still remaining in touch with the depressed feelings and the crisis that precipitated the request for treatment.

The therapist must provide hope for the client based on the conviction that the client can take responsibility for proactive behavior—making decisions and using the ego's executive functions. The client may have great difficulty in believing that a gay person can be self-actualized and may try to enlist the counselor in feelings of hopelessness and helplessness. As a result, the unwary worker may have an impulse to take over, engage in very generalized reassurances, give advice, or adopt a cheer-up attitude. However, the counselor must realize that no advice can be given that the client hasn't already considered and negated with rationalizations and that the client has already been told to cheer up more than is tolerable.

In addition to providing hope, active listening is necessary. The depressed client has usually said that no one listens or that he or she has had negative interactions with others who have not been able to tolerate the depression. Significant persons may have given advice, tried to cheer the client, or tried to divert the client's attention from the depression. The worker should help the client to finish thoughts. For example:

Client: I just feel . . . .
Worker: Yes?
Client: That I can't go on.
Worker: Go on where or doing what?
Client: Feeling this way.
Worker: Feeling what way?
Client: That I'm gay.
Worker: What does that mean to you?
Client: That I'm no good.
Worker: How does being gay mean that you're no good?

This illustrates how the worker can return to the underlying issue of internalized negative stereotypes. The client's feelings are "If the stereotypes are right and if that is indeed what I am, then there's no hope for me to be what I really think or know I am." The worker's responsibility is again to help the client examine and find constructive ways to act on reality. Both people can explore the reasons for not having implemented alternatives to stereotypes, and the client may be helped to resolve conflicts that prevented him or her from using good ideas about self.

The client must be able to express the guilt and anger that are the underlying dynamics for depression. Gays have been taught that they should not exist and may have felt but not expressed anger about such teachings. They also may feel guilty about continuing to live and when the anger and guilt are seen as bad and are not allowed expression, they are turned inward. The counselor must permit the client to feel and express these emotions. The client should also be helped to see the ineffectiveness of alcohol or drug abuse in dealing with depression. This applies particularly to alcohol which is likely to intensify the depression rather than to alleviate it.

With the counselor's support in bringing feelings to the surface, the client can move to constructive action and away from rumination, guilt, and nonpurposeful activity. Such action necessarily involves decision making that will support life goals and an identity as a gay person. Client and worker should begin to identify support systems that will reflect and promote a positive gay self-identity. It is important to remember that one of the predominant aspects of crisis is the feeling of loss of all familiar supports. Therefore, the counselor may need to help the client locate new supports. For example, the worker can locate existing systems in the community that support an alternative life-style. It is not enough to verify the existence of a women's center; one must know its degree of acceptance of lesbians. Additionally, the worker can actually call and verify the times, dates, and places of gay coalition meetings and might even go with the client to a meeting or two if the client fears joining a new group without immediate support. When one has previously encountered rejection, it is common to feel uncertain. Regarding old support systems, the worker may now be able to work with the client and significant others to increase mutual esteem.

Finally, the worker has a responsibility to work with the client well beyond the resolution of guilt feelings. Identifying the good things about being gay is equally important. Among these are the increased sensitivity that self-aware gays, as members of an oppressed minority, can have for other persons and the gratification that comes from living and enjoying sex without anxiety. Also important is socializing with other gays and the joy of self-esteem that accrues from finding support systems that accept one for the totality of self and not for behaving only in prescribed ways. From such experiences can emerge a true sense of one's own individuality.

Throughout this section, the authors have reiterated that not all clients suffer from crisis to the same degree or proceed through each stage. We also caution that the interventive processes identified are not a recipe or an exhaustive list of all that can be done. The intent has been to provide guidelines for problem solving.

Also, coming out to self may solve the problem presented by the client and may permit self-fulfillment in living and loving relationships. However, full self-actualization has other aspects with which the client will deal later in life as a gay person. Such self-actualization may be accomplished without professional help, and the worker should convey a sense of faith in the client's reality-based strengths, an acceptance of the client's ability to use old and new problem solving skills, and an acceptance of the client's choices about how he or she will live a gay life-style. The worker should also make clear that he or she is available for future help.

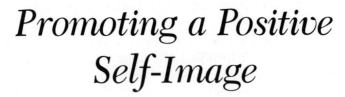

4

Promoting a Positive Self-Image

The problems of coming out described in Chapter Three are frequently grouped under the label "homosexual crisis." Most gays encounter this stress to some degree, and any anxiety caused by it may lead them to seek help. Not all gay clients experience an identity crisis, but those who have internalized self-acceptance by themselves or in counseling still have other issues to resolve. Therapeutic intervention at this stage involves actualizing a gay identity sexually and socially. The second phase of coming out to self requires clarification of sentiments and decisions about how self-definition will find social validation. The client moves from a focus on coping with internal emotions to concerns about how such feelings will be acted on and received by others.

The fact that a homosexual identity is stigmatized places gay persons in a discredited social position and creates dilemmas for them (Goffman, 1963), even if they positively identify with their homosexuality.

Other people may react negatively if they are aware of this identity. Even before coming out to others, the gay person must resolve personal conflicts about personal meanings related to a gay identity and about how his or her daily behavior reflects the total self. Unfortunately, there are relatively few situations where these issues can be discussed in depth and in relationship to the cognitive integration of feelings and behavior. Decisive choice of a gay life-style occurs only after problems related to self-definition have been resolved. Viewing gayness only as a handicap ignores the role of sexuality in the individual's total personality. Sexual orientation is a key element in establishing identity and determining social behavior. To believe that sexuality is any less an issue for homosexuals than for heterosexuals is patently ridiculous. Defining the sentiments held about sexual preference is essential.

Coming out to self in a self-actualizing manner can be expressed as progression from "Yes, I'm gay and that's OK" to "Now what do I do?" The new therapeutic goal is concerned with developing a set of personal meanings for a positive sense of self. Two major factors inhibit such efforts. First, the gay individual may have only been exposed to the negative stereotypes projected by society. A second and closely related concern is that the stereotypes may have created fear of relationships and isolation that inhibits efforts to explore self-identity.

The therapeutic issues thus have a strong interactional focus. For this reason, group counseling is preferable to individual counseling for several reasons. Use of the group offers structured interaction with other gay people and helps to break down social isolation. If the group is sufficiently heterogeneous in terms of sex, age, and experience, all members will be exposed to a broad array of insights and possible behaviors for living a creative gay life-style. Also, support and mutual respect can greatly assist each member to test new insights and to clarify understanding of self before acting on them outside of the group. Finally, a heterogeneous group of gays can make up for deficiencies in or the insensitivity of counselors who are not fully aware of the diversities within gay culture.

The Problem of Stereotypes

From a developmental perspective, studies such as that by Kinsey and others (1948) and a survey of gay psychologists ("Removing the

Stigma," 1977), indicate that the awareness of homoerotic feelings and incidental homosexual behavior are likely to precede a homosexual identity. Clinical experience indicates that the period between awareness of homoerotic feelings and self-identity is frequently filled with fear, denial, and withdrawal as one's feelings are in increasing contrast with homophobic stereotypes. As one's feelings become more apparent and more forceful, self-identification as homosexual can no longer be denied. This can lead to self-hate, even greater fear, and social isolation because of the fear of discovery. Unfortunately, such self-imposed isolation, particularly in regard to sexual orientation, may increase acceptance of homophobic stereotypes. Homoerotically oriented individuals may feel that they have no choice but to act out the stereotypes.

During a group therapy session, Thomas explained with amusement what he called his "Nelly phase," It was a period of time shortly after he had accepted his same-sex orientation; he went to considerable effort to wear women's clothes and to affect effeminate mannerisms. Alan retorted that he found such behavior reprehensible because it gave gay men a bad name. Ann in turn wondered why Thomas would have ever wanted to act so curiously. Thomas, somewhat surprised at the negative responses that he received, replied, "But I just thought that was what I was *supposed* to do."

Although the circumstances and the behaviors adopted may vary, Thomas' situation is not unusual. Frequently the knowledge of the gay person who has been isolated is confined to homophobic stereotypes. This, in turn, may prompt self-destructive behavior. Behavior based upon such ignorance and the negative experiences that result from it inhibit the development of a positive, mature sexual self-expression and increase a sense of self-negation and shame. Even when such behavior is motivated by an angry decision to flout society, the momentary catharsis may be overcome by the long-term negative effects.

An additional problem is the tendency to generalize these negative stereotypes to other aspects of self-image. For example, during a group session, Keith complained that he was not attractive to other gay men whom he felt were all hung up on an extremely masculine image. Several group members contested this view, but Keith persisted. To substantiate his claim, he said that when he went to gay bars, no one ever looked at him with interest. Thus, he felt very undesirable. Again, the group members strongly dissented. They pointed out that gay men's tastes in other men were as varied as the men themselves. Other members pointed out that they found Keith attractive. These comments made the handsome young man quite uncomfortable, and he protested that the group was just trying to make him feel better. As the differences between Keith's self-image and how he was viewed by the others was pursued, it became apparent that although Keith intellectually identified himself as gay and accepted his affectional preference, residual negative feelings were being manifested in his opinion of his physical appearance. Early religious training had taught him that homosexual behavior was a sin and that he was therefore bad. In turn, the unresolved sense of being bad had been generalized into an unrealistic view of himself as being ugly.

All gay persons become aware of the negative images of their life-style. One result of this awareness is anger and rejection of all stereotypes. Frequently the painful realization is then made that some aspects of what has been rejected have been internalized to a surprising degree. Few gays are immune to the influence of these negative stereotypes, whether they are proudly proclaiming that they are gay or beginning to define their identity. That is, stereotyping of gays is not just a heterosexual's problem in relating to gays but an issue for homosexuals interacting with other gays. Thus, the problem of stereotyping among gays must also be considered in counseling.

Clark (1977) has described intervention related to negative stereotypes as the process of deprogramming. Society has projected these negative stereotypes in order to establish negative associations with gayness. In effect, gay individuals have been brainwashed, and the grip of these stereotypes must be broken before gays can make any substantial progress toward developing a positive self-identity. The process of intervention in a group setting can focus on two areas: the stereotypes themselves and their impact on the gay persons' identities. During discussion, the facilitator must ensure that the group deals sufficiently with each issue. Regarding the first area, the participants must understand the nature and social purpose of stereotypes. Regarding the second, the participants must realize how such images have affected the behavior of gays in general and the behavior and attitudes of each individual.

In discussing negative stereotypes, the discussion frequently flows from point to point. The following is a hypothetical interaction that shows this flow with respect to the two areas just identified.

Facilitator:	Can you think of a stereotype about gays that particularly bugs you?
John:	Yeah, they think that we're all limp-wristed faggots!
Peter:	We're just as macho as straight guys.
Other group members:	Yeah. Yeah.
Alan:	Jeez, I went to San Francisco for Gay Pride Week and the march. I got out of the march, though. You should have seen all of the sissies prancing around, looking like fools. I was really embarrassed.
Thomas:	Hey, wait a minute! What are you getting down on those guys for? I mean, just because it isn't your thing . . .
Alan:	Well, hell, they give us all a bad name. How are we ever going to get straight people to accept us with them flitting around?
Thomas:	So, I suppose you want us all to get into your macho number.
Kenneth:	Well, I can't help how I look.
Alan:	Hey, Kenny, don't get me wrong. I didn't mean . . .
Kenneth:	Well, you are putting me down. After all, I'd look pretty silly all done up in a lumber jacket and boots number.
Bert:	Bullshit! All you sissies give me a pain.
Carl:	Hey, ease up Bert!
Thomas:	This is too much. I mean don't we have enough trouble without tearing each other apart?
Alan:	Hey! Let's cool it. I mean I didn't figure on starting a fight!

The deprogramming effort was started by asking the group to pick out a stereotype of gays that disturbed them. Group members frequently tend to begin discussion on an abstract level, which is less threatening. However, once a particular stereotype has been chosen, individual and personal reactions must be dealt with. Initially the stereotype is totally rejected ("We're just as macho as straight guys.") Rather than letting the group avoid confrontation, the facilitator can lead the discussion toward issues such as how the stereotype started and why heterosexuals need to believe it. Mentioning that the stereotypes often represent the opposite of idealized heterosexual behavior is helpful. For instance, in the example, effeminate behavior is the central issue. Related questions would be: "Is this a negative characteristic?" "Do attitudes against effeminate behavior impinge upon an effeminate individual's sense of self-worth?" "Why is there in-group anger toward the effeminate group member?" "What distinction can be made between genuine behavioral traits and minstralized behavior?" "Why do gays often act out the most negative stereotypes?"

In later group sessions, participants are likely to realize that the simple rejection of the stereotypes does not eliminate all the problems associated with them. At this point, the discussion should focus on self. The pertinent question is "How does this stereotype affect me as an individual?" In the example, three patterns of reaction are noticeable. First, anger was displayed toward gays who manifest the stereotyped behaviors; second, repressed feelings of guilt and shame surfaced; and finally, discussion of what is appropriate behavior and who is the judge evoked anger and confusion. Each of these patterns offers effective interventive points for the facilitator if other group members have not already picked up on them. Examining these particular areas demands that the clients clarify meanings. Every negative stereotype implies a heterosexist ideal that should be identified and examined. Does the ideal have any validity? For example, is a man any less a man because of effeminate behavior?

Having assessed and then rejected or accepted the accuracy of these implicit heterosexist ideals, their appropriateness within a homosexual life-style should be addressed. For example, appropriate questions may be: "Is the heterosexual idea of long-term monogamous relationships appropriate for gays?" "What is the basis for projecting the ideal of long-term relationships onto a gay life-style?" If the behavioral ideal is deemed inappropriate, what related behavior is more appropriate and why? Such a discussion reinforces the fact that a variety of behaviors may be appropriate within a gay life-style.

The group members can then establish principles for their own actions. Within the group, each client can determine his or her own behavioral ideals. The clients should focus on self within a social matrix. That is, they should help each other perceive identity as related to interpersonal relationships. The clients can then generalize from acceptance of self to acceptance of others. For example, the problem of what will be judged as appropriate for the client will rest in whether particular senti- ments and behaviors are personally and socially fulfilling or whether they are destructive to self or others. The behavior of other persons should be evaluated according to the same criteria.

Self-Definition

Inherent in the principles of action just delineated is the develop- ment of a sense of empowerment, which may be defined as the capacity to identify and use inner resources in creative and assertive self-actuali- zation. Dealing with the negative stereotypes should help participants understand the degree to which they have allowed themselves to be de- fined by others. Additionally, this examination should motivate the members toward self-definition as they realize that freeing oneself from the oppression of stereotypes is not enough. Though there may be a great sense of freedom resulting from what has been accomplished, no effort to provide a blueprint for proactive self-actualization has been made. The basic goal at this stage is to establish personal sentiments and values that can be principles for a creative life-style. For example, since sexual behavior has traditionally been the focus of a gay identity, how will the client decide what sexual behaviors will express his or her feelings about self and others? Related questions are: "Will sexual behavior be the total of my self-definition, of my gayness? If not, what am I seeking to express by my sexual behavior? Does my behavior convey this intent?"

Clients must be able to discuss sexual behavior openly and directly. Societal pressures have generally forced gay people to suppress their sexual feelings. As the new sense of freedom and personal empowerment begins to have its effect, a strong need to express these feelings develops. Unlike heterosexuals, who are able to process both feelings and sexual behaviors during their developmental years, gays are likely to find that the group provides the first such opportunity to do so. Providing an ac- cepting and open milieu for such interchanges is extremely important. The following situation demonstrates the need for self-definition relative to sexuality.

At a group session, Alan vividly described his sexual exploits in public parks. After listening for some time, Thomas exploded in anger.

Thomas:	Shit, Alan, is that all you're interested in? Getting your rocks off?
Alan:	Well, what's wrong with that?
Thomas:	Everything, man! I mean, if that's all sex means to you, why don't you stay home and masturbate?
Facilitator:	Hey, Thomas! You're angry. Why?
Thomas:	All Alan does is use people!

The stage was now set for an extensive discussion of how members of the group viewed their sexual behavior: Why did they choose to express their sexual feelings in the ways they did? What did these choices mean to them and to their partners? What did they wish to express? Was what they did consistent with what they wished to express? Long-established habits of repression, denial, and fear have often crippled the ability to move away from passively accepting prohibition against discussion of homosexual behaviors. Other pertinent questions could evolve from the discussion. The purpose is to investigate present activities in light of desired self-definitions. Clients are frequently perplexed at their initial inability to assess the meaning of sexuality and its expression. The invidious influences of social isolation, stigmatization, unconscious internalization of negative self-images, and past negative experiences have conspired to place many gays in a defensive and uncertain position. As a result, participants often find that they have not developed their gay identity beyond a vague understanding of it as something they have. Gayness is not perceived as an identity from which to act and derive positive meaning in their lives.

Three basic questions form the core of discussions that seek to break the oppressive bonds of definition by others and to develop and assert personalized positive meanings and behaviors.

1. What does being gay mean to me now?
2. What do I want my gay identity to mean?
3. What am I going to do to achieve my desired identity?

Because of the passive-reactive stance taken by many gays, leading up to the question "What does being gay mean to me now?" may take a while. A helpful modality is an exercise of free association. Participants are given a paper with the sentence "I am gay, therefore I . . . ." They are then asked to complete the sentence with ten verbs or verb phrases as quickly as possible. The list should include behaviors that are considered both positive and negative. For this reason, an atmosphere of support and assistance must be firmly established and sustained. The words and phrases are then shared, forming the basis for analyzing the sentiments as the clients see them manifested in their behaviors. If clients behave in certain ways, they must have personal reasons. This is not a time for blaming but for discovering and understanding what knowledge and values form the basis of the individual's actions.

During a group session, Ann expressed a great deal of discomfort in explicitly discussing sexual activity. She firmly refused to define her relationship with Mary only in sexual terms. She found the talk about sex distasteful because sex was only a small part of who she was.

Tom pointed out, somewhat defensively, that sex must be fairly important because Ann's sexual preference seemed to bring her to the group sessions each week. Ann retorted that sexuality was a part of her but that it was not very important. Other group members picked up on her defensiveness, seeking reasons for it and noting that she seemed to be pushing her sexual person off to the side. Subsequent discussions revealed that when Ann was a teenager, she and a girl friend had been discovered having sex by her mother, who almost became hysterical. After learning that the two girls had been involved for several months, her mother forbade any association. In addition, Ann was sent to her clergyman, who lectured her about the sinfulness and unnaturalness of homosexual behavior. Gradually, as the discussion continued, Ann began to realize that although she accepted her affectional preference, even to the point of forming a committed relationship with Mary, the fear and shame she had experienced had caused her to repress and compartmentalize her sexual expression to such a degree that she reluctantly engaged in sex and only at Mary's urgings. Group members challenged this behavior, insisting that sexual activity should be an important part of how gays express their love for one another. They wondered how Mary must feel about Ann's attitudes about sex. Mary admitted that they had never really talked about them. Ann agreed to talk to Mary about sexuality between group sessions. The following meeting Mary and Ann arrived together and announced that indeed they had done a great deal of talking about the sexual aspect of their relationship. Ann had been surprised to learn that Mary had been both frustrated and hurt by her reluctance. Mary had begun to see it as a sign of Ann's lack of affection for her and was worried about whether their relationship would last.

The first steps toward reintegrating Ann's sexuality with her love for Mary had been taken. Now Ann was more aware of Mary's needs and her responsibility to be sensitive to them. For the first time, she considered the effects that the traumatic experience of her youth had had on her. Although she previously thought it best to forget the incident, it proved to be largely responsible for the attitudes that she had internalized. By confronting this incident, she gradually came to understand her feelings and behavior. The effort was painful, but the love and support of Mary and the rest of the group made it rewarding. Past experiences affect present values, attitudes, and behavior. Understanding present behavior demands that its origins be analyzed.

The following provides a framework for problem solving:

> If I and others who understand me and my life-style find my present behavior constructive and self-actualizing, understanding the meanings that motivate that behavior enhances my ability to apply those meanings to other choices in the future.
>
> If I and others find my behavior destructive to self or others, understanding the negative meanings that motivate that behavior helps me to change those meanings or to increase my understanding so that I can adopt more creative and self-actualizing behavior.
>
> If I am uncertain about the meanings that motivate my behavior because of repression or projection, then I am acting stupidly.
>
> I must bring to the surface old ideas or create new meanings for my behaviors.

Acceptance by others is a vital issue to gays, particularly for those who are just coming out. As such, the social trap of being a "good gay" is always present. Being a good gay means not living a life-style that in any way will make nongays conscious of the person as a gay. This dynamic, though subtle, is destructive. While appearing to accept the gay individual, disapproval of any overt behavior that validates self-identity is communicated. As a result, the counselor has a unique opportunity to help explore avenues for proactive, self-actualizing behavior.

Up to this point, the focus has been on how the past affects the present. Clients must develop a firm understanding and belief that their values and attitudes are not bound either to the past or the present. Clients can be, through their own empowerment and the support of others, the creators of their futures. The central question becomes "What do I want my gay identity to mean to me?" The facilitator should constantly reinforce the principle that the group members have the power to decide who they will be if they make their own decisions and act upon them. Understanding and accepting that challenge are the next steps to liberated and meaningfully creative behavior. Self-definition must not be influenced by others who do not share in the sense of selfhood. The focus must be on the individual self and those who share in creating the gay identity. The client is then free to be who he or she wants to be.

Proactive self-definition can begin with fantasy exercises geared to free the participants from the past and present. One approach is to send the group on a fantasy trip. Everyone enters a rocket ship and eventually lands on a perfect planet populated only by gay people. Questions to be answered are: "What would it be like?" "How would the people act?" "How would you live and act there?" Discussion lies primarily with the last question. After discussing the first two questions, the participants jot down their thoughts about the final question. The first two questions are intended to make the participants think about an ideal order unaffected by worldly realities. The final question provides the basis for conceptualizing the ideal self. Unrestricted fantasizing is helpful since habits of repression are relinquished with difficulty and may block the visualization of ideal self. The old adage of "Be gay if you must, but be careful" dies hard. Inhibition must be counteracted by encouragement to fantasize, regardless of how ridiculous or impossible the dreams may be.

The discussions should offer ample opportunity to bring the ideal self back into the world by making the necessary reality adjustments. As the individuals' ideal selves take shape, the facilitator should reinforce them by pointing out aspects that are already present in the individuals and that can be enhanced. The participants should be encouraged to think of ways to develop those aspects that they do not see as being a part of themselves. Members are also encouraged to share one another's ideals. The original list of each person can be worked on so that it becomes a realistic, positive profile of who each person wishes to become. Certain cautions should be exercised, however. First, rigid expectations about meeting one's ideal self-image should be avoided. Participants must understand that an ideal is just that and thus should always be open to modification. Second, the ideal should be brought into a realistic perspective.

The objective is not to project a "super gay" person but rather to create reasonable goals that will make the individual's gay life-style creative and productive.

No one can simply wish an ideal self into being; it must be acted upon. The focus becomes how does each client achieve the desired identity. If appropriate goals have been chosen, the participants, with mutual support and encouragement, should want to establish that identity in their everyday social lives. Because such an effort should not be left to chance, a plan of action is needed. The group setting offers the clients the opportunity to share and test plans of action before they act independently outside of the group.

Some specific questions that should be addressed include:

1. On which goal or goals do I wish to focus at the present time?
2. Whose support will help me achieve my goal?
3. What are the possible obstacles to success?
4. How do I plan to enlist the support that I feel will be helpful, and how do I plan to deal with the obstacles?

The key to these questions is focusing one's efforts. Each ideal will seem good and therefore deserving of immediate attention. However, to work toward all of them simultaneously would dissipate one's energy, leading to failure, frustration, and a loss of self-esteem. Analyzing supports and anticipated obstacles can help to establish realistic priorities. For example, a participant may establish the goal of finding a stable, monogamous relationship. Realistically, a necessary prior step may be the development of appropriate social contacts. Here, other group members can help by mentioning gay organizations or gay friends outside of the therapy group. Planning helps prevent hasty, self-defeating actions.

The group offers mutual support and assistance to each member as each becomes more active as a gay person in diverse social settings. Since group members are likely to be disappointed when their efforts are not immediately successful, participants should choose initial goals that are relatively easy to achieve. In the example related to developing social contacts, it might be advisable for the participant to pick a particular gay organization within which there can be a sense of contribution based on personal assets and start regular participation in activities. Establishing support systems is extremely important. Besides the more obvious benefit of enhancing goal attainment, they also help clients to become more active with others who share or understand and reinforce their personal goals. Weinberg and Williams (1975) stress that the existence of such support systems is positively correlated with a healthy gay life-style.

The fact that most of society is not ready to facilitate in establishing alternative sexual-affectional identities is one reason why creating gay support systems is necessary. Many of a client's previous contacts may reject or grudgingly tolerate the gay person's open identity. They may wish to maintain a relationship with the person they once knew but feel either incapable or unwilling to support the "new self."

Specific actions for implementing plans might, at first glance, seem unnecessary. However, the need for such concreteness is proportionate to the degree of negative self-image and social isolation with which clients enter the therapeutic setting. For example, a significant number of self-referred clients have found that even after deciding to take part in the group sessions, actually attending is very difficult. Therefore, specific activities prevent members from being inactive as they attempt to move out from the relative support and security of the therapy group. Two activities in particular have been found to be very helpful for the group at this time. Grace (1977) and Clark (1977) each point out the benefits of assertiveness training. We also found that actual "scripting" and role playing of an anticipated effort is often helpful in enhancing social skills.

As the participant tests minor tasks successfully and receives group reinforcement, he or she can generalize the efforts to ever-widening social situations. Within the therapeutic context, the individual is helped to reaffirm the appropriateness of acting as a person who is gay and to reflect qualities of self-actualization such as true individuality and self-sufficiency.

5

Exploring Dilemmas of Social Acceptance

The presenting problem of the gay client at this stage of identity development may be stated as: "I am gay. I like being gay and living as a gay person, but these facts affect others in my world. I'm not alone, so what do I do now?" Realistic problem solving directed toward creative living cannot be confined to self-definition. With the client having achieved the conscious and cohesive sentiments that define a gay identity, the key element of the next phase of the therapeutic process is to explore new relationships and activities that will provide support for continued self-development. Ernest Becker (1964, p. 261) summed up the general issue: "Man needs man in order to discover and validate his own inner powers, in order to unfold himself; he needs to *see* and experience man in order to be convinced that there is absolute meaning in nature."

Homophobic social pressures, however, may severely inhibit many clients from socially asserting a gay identity. If homoerotic feelings and needs are only fatalistically acknowledged, these needs are likely to be expressed in self-alienating and self-destructive ways. For example, Terry informed the group one evening that he did not see what all the fuss was about regarding coming out. As far as he was concerned, his homosexuality was just a part of who he was. When he needed sex, a pickup off the streets or in the park could always offer quick, safe, anonymous sex. Subsequent discussion elicited the fact that sexual interaction under such circumstances was anything but safe—one could be arrested and even physically assaulted or robbed. When Terry acknowledged these facts but said that the risks were probably worth taking, the basic issue gradually surfaced. Tom questioned Terry's need for anonymity. At this point, Terry revealed the humiliation that he would feel if his family and friends learned that he was a homosexual.

The problem is the conflict between the need to assert what is viewed as a worthwhile self and the fear of rejection. The dilemma is that the more positively gay persons feel about themselves and the more they integrate their sexual-affectional preference, the more dissatisfied they become with not being totally open about themselves with the people who matter to them most. Hiding a gay identity when it is the source of conflict or shame is one thing, but hiding it when it is accepted as a positive aspect of oneself is incongruent and must be rectified by the client. Inevitably, the gay person must come out to others to some degree.

Such interaction is, as Sidney Jourard (1971, p. 32) points out, essential to good mental health and growth: "I say that self-disclosure is a means by which one achieves personality health. I mean it is not until I am my real self and I act my real self that my real self is in a position to grow. Every maladjusted person is a person who has not made himself known to another human being and in consequence does not know himself. Nor can he be himself. More than that he struggles actively to avoid becoming known by another human being."

The goal of therapy at this point is to help the client initiate a breadth of significant relationships as a gay person. A therapeutic group will eventually be unable to meet these relationship needs because it is relatively closed and limited in resources. A healthy life-style demands a variety of social inputs if problems are to be avoided or resolved. Issues related to coming out to others can be viewed within two social environments: other gays and the broader society, which consists primarily of heterosexuals. The problem-solving process revolves around four questions which can relate to either context:

1.   Why should I or why do I want to assert my gay identity?
2.   With whom should I assert my gay identity?
3.   How should I assert my gay identity?
4.   When and where should I assert my gay identity?

A group approach has been found to be beneficial not only during the development of a positive gay identity but also during the period of identity assertion. The group should focus the four basic questions identified above and in that order. The group offers a safe and supportive atmosphere in which each participant can determine and test a personal social plan of action. However, the facilitator must ensure that the group does not become an end in itself. Despite anticipated hostility from the world at large, participants should be encouraged to test decisions made in the group beyond its boundaries. Particularly in the early stages, but throughout the life of the group, members should show evidence of action in the normal social environment and should be encouraged to seek out, develop, and integrate into gay support systems outside of the group. Reviewing these efforts should be a regular part of the meetings, because the goal during this problem-solving period is to make the therapy group ultimately unnecessary by establishing a variety of social interactions.

The Need for Self-Assertion

A gay identity is a social identity, and living a gay life-style demands interacting in society at large. If the individual is self-identified as gay, that reality will affect interactions, regardless of the person's intent. Since the motives and quality of assertion are largely determined by the personal attitudes toward gayness, the group should identify and share these attitudes first. The initial decision making and problem solving by the group participants should be related to the question: "Why should I or why do I want to assert my gay identity?" The facilitator should understand that *what* will be asserted is essential. The time spent by the group discussing why they should assert their gay identity will vary according to the degree to which participants have clarified their self-identities. If group participants have already done the problem solving described in the previous chapter, the facilitator can lead an inventory exercise as a means of reinforcement. This can be a homework task in which group participants make lists of what being gay means to them. At the next meeting, each member reads and explains his or her list to the others. If a new group is being formed to deal with the issue of coming out to others, the facilitator must provide sufficient time to elicit, clarify, and reinforce attitudes toward gayness felt by the participants. The exercises provided previously can help in this effort.

When the facilitator and the group feel that these sentiments are sufficiently established, the discussion can focus on why positive feedback from acquaintances is important to a sense of well-being. It has been found helpful to address first the need for validation outside of the area of sexual-affectional identity. Most group members can describe having been afraid of self-disclosure because of homophobic or repressive experiences but still taking a chance in coming out to a significant other and being warmly accepted. After briefly exploring reactions to repression, contrasts can be made to the experiences and feelings after self-expression. In this manner, the principle of validation through action is firmly established and reinforced, and the facilitator can discuss validation regarding sexual-affectional identity. In discussing the assertion of gay identity, initial attention should be those life experiences that were positive and validating. Discussing these experiences can form the basis for later discussion about whom a gay identity should be shared with. For example, many gays have felt great self-esteem when they asserted their identities to themselves. Assertion of identity in the group can be another instance of validation. Most gay individuals have experienced considerable rejection and pain because of their gayness, so the facilitator should be careful not to overemphasize negative and alienating experiences. However, such experiences will need to be dealt with when they counter-balance the need for validation.

Each participant needs to understand the need for identity assertion and then must commit self to social interaction as a gay person. Each participant should remember that he or she has the power and responsibility to recognize, define, and act on personal sentiments that should govern and motivate assertion of a unique gay identity. Each participant has the responsibility to evaluate social behavior and its consistency with desired sentiments and behaviors. Each participant should seek to validate these through conscious, selective social action.

The effects of permitting homophobic people to limit or determine appropriate behavior also have to be explored by participants. Local ordinances that prohibit gay bars or coffee houses or same sex individuals from renting one bedroom apartments or restrict employment opportunities limit the social contexts where gay men and women can assert their total identities. In essence, such acts of social denial invalidate gay people. Although the gay liberation movement and the more enlightened professional view of homosexual behavior have lessened the likelihood of gays viewing themselves as sick, bad, or crazy, it is increasingly important that gays come out so as to counter the shift of focus among homophobics to the social context. Gays should assert their rights to be total persons and to act as total persons, because the battle of social and civil rights cannot be effectively waged from the closet, and nongays cannot be expected to win the battle for gays.

The group context provides a setting for testing reactions to homophobia and for implementing assertive strategies. For example, Ann arrived at a group meeting very upset. Although she and her partner had recently decided to move to a new, larger apartment and had found what they both wanted, the landlord objected to their lesbian relationship. They also learned that they had no legal recourse. In the discussion, it became clear that the hurt and anger felt by Ann were shared by the others and that those feelings arouse as much because a good and valid relationship was denied as because the right to self-identity as lesbian was denigrated. The incident could have had negative effects both on Ann's sense of identity and on her relationship.

John expressed similar anger and frustration about the professional dilemma that his gay identity created for him. As a teacher, John was very popular among his minority students. They had said that he seemed to understand their feelings better than the other white teachers and had asked why this was so. He responded vaguely, which had a harmful effect on the good rapport that they had all enjoyed. Because of the oppressive circumstances of his job, John could not tell these students that perhaps his understanding arose from the fact that he, too, was a member of an oppressed group. What could have been a positive and constructive learning situation became, because of a homophobic milieu, a frustrating and negative experience of non-communication.

These examples illustrate the legal and social problems of being gay in a homophobic society and the difficult decisions involved in coming out to others. However, an identity, particularly a positive, creative identity, requires sharing if it is to grow, and the counselor can use the group process to meet this need.

After discussing the reasons for identity assertion, the group then considers to whom one asserts. The group facilitator must have a realistic outlook in this regard. Although the ideal is to be out to everyone, this is not always advantageous. For example, one should not reveal one's gayness to individuals who would react maliciously. Neither should the gay person come out because of a desire to punish parents, other relatives, old friends, or other gays.

Tom told the group that he had been considering telling his father of his gay identity. On one hand, he felt a real need to let his father know. On the other hand, he was very fearful of how his father would react. When asked why he was so fearful, Tom stated that he, Tom, had taken a long time to consider himself an "OK person," but his father felt that Tom had never done anything right. In intervening, the therapist guided Tom into considering the destructive nature of the father-son relationship. Tom needed to consider whether revealing his gay identity was merely setting himself up for more of the same. Would asserting his gay identity at this time serve any positive purpose for either him or his father?

A general rule of thumb is that one should come out to another person if it is likely to help the relationship. In weighing the possible outcome, gay clients should be encouraged to ask themselves if the self-disclosure is important to their ability to self-actualize. No simple formula fits all relationships and all situations. Each instance must be judged individually, and, the facilitator and the other group members can help provide guidance and assistance in this analysis.

Coming Out to Gays

A first step in asserting and validating a gay identity beyond the therapeutic group might be to do so to other gays. The counselor must understand that coming out is more difficult for individuals who have only recently accepted their gay identities. Fear of social stigma causes much of gay life to be invisible. Members of the group who are more familiar with local gay society should be encouraged to help other participants by suggesting various social meeting places and by introducing those who are just coming out to other gays.

The group facilitator should also be familiar with social and recreational opportunities. An overly restricted social environment can create problems, as exemplified in the following case. Ellen and Helen came to a counselor, complaining that their relationship of five years was falling apart. Helen stated with tears that they only sniped at each other and that nothing seemed to please Ellen any more. Ellen angrily accused Helen of picking fights over "the littlest things." The counselor asked the couple what kinds of social things they did together. The women mentioned only occasional movies and concerts. When the counselor asked about activities with other couples, they both stated that they never would think of doing such a thing. Absolutely no one knew about the full nature of their relationship. They were convinced that if they became involved with other gay people, nongays would find out. As a result, several important friendships would probably end, and they would be likely to lose their jobs.

One of the problems indicated here is a relatively closed environment in which Ellen and Helen can assert and validate their gay identities. The closed nature of the relationship also precluded any constructive input or constructive output. Ellen and Helen needed to recognize the need for inputs and to trust themselves and others in social relationships. They needed to explore the kinds of relationships they desired and with whom they could develop relationships based on mutual interests.

In testing their ability to relate within a gay environment, clients are likely to become aware that past attitudes and patterns of behavior persist despite efforts to shed negative stereotypes and to adopt a positive attitude. Peter came to a group meeting feeling very dejected and angry. His doctor had informed Peter that afternoon that he had contracted venereal warts. His anger was directed at the unknown person who had given him the disease and caused him the embarrassment. The members of the group pointed out that as long as he insisted on seeking out anonymous sexual contacts in bars and baths, he had to accept the consequences. Peter protested that as a liberated gay, he should be free to pursue his sexual pleasures as he saw fit. Some group members challenged his definition of liberated behavior, wondering if his anonymous sex was merely a way of using others who were not so clear about their own identities. Was his activity perhaps just a subtle way of negating his own and others' homosexuality? The group then examined positive gay sexual-affectional life-styles.

In moving out from the group environment into the larger gay culture, clients will quickly learn or be reminded that they will not always be greeted with the same support and concern. As with any life-style, there are positive and negative aspects; some people are good, and some are bad, and there are creative and destructive dynamics. The discrepancies between the ideal world desired by gays who are coming out and the real world often generate considerable anger. It can be particularly galling when "one of your own kind" uses or exploits a kindred soul. Andy expressed these feelings when he confronted Alan during a group meeting. During the previous week, Andy had gone to one of the local gay bars, where he had met Alan. During their conversation, a very effeminate young man came up to Alan and expressed a great deal of affection. After the young man left, Alan remarked, "Oh, he's great in bed, but I wouldn't want to be seen in the supermarket with him." Other group members made Alan aware of his exploitative behavior.

The facilitator should encourage members to process negative experiences that occur while the members are entering into gay activities. Otherwise, clients who have developed an idealized vision of their gay lifestyle may be discouraged and withdraw from the group or any other gay relationships. While the therapist should seek to accentuate positive experiences, it is equally important to resolve setbacks. For instance, it is important to reinforce the fact that relationships will vary in intensity and character as they do in society at large. Candy came to a group meeting very depressed and angry. In the previous two sessions she had glowingly described Janice, a new friend whom she had met at the local gay caucus meeting. Their involvement had deepened rapidly, and Candy had decided that she had found Ms. Right. However, during the past weekend, Janice had dashed Candy's dreams, saying that although she liked Candy very much as a friend, she had no interest in forming an exclusive relationship. Candy believed that Janice had led her on and was now rejecting her. She had stormed from Janice's house, vowing never to have anything to do with her again.

In the processing that followed, Candy gradually became aware of the fact that her expectations for an intense, exclusive relationship were unrealistic. Such a relationship is best built mutually over a period of time and not overnight. Group members questioned Candy as to whether she was actually the rejecting person, since she could not have her way. Janice had not rejected her but had only defined the relationship within what she considered reasonable bounds. The problem for Candy was whether she was willing to accept a less intense relationship. The worker and group members made clear that every relationship in a gay life-style need not be a love affair and need not be sexualized.

Coming Out to Nongays

The problems concerned with coming out to heterosexuals are frequently the most difficult. Most of the client's significant others are nongays, and their reactions to a gay identity are least predictable. Much of the sense of release or even exuberance that may have been felt as the client asserted a gay identity among gays quickly fades when confronted with the issues and problems of self-revelation to nongays, and a high level of fear and anxiety about negative responses is likely. These significant others had a primary influence on the client's personal development, but they also helped to establish the client's negative self-image.

Out of a mixture of love, fear and survival, gays often create a web of deceit about their sexual-affectional nature. One client described the dilemma by stating, "Once I told the 'Big Lie,' the rest of the lies just kept coming." People who have played the most significant roles in the gay person's self-image and whose opinions remain most significant often do not know that the client is gay. Consequently, the issue of openness implies that past relationships have been based on fraud. The more developed one's sense of gay identity, the greater the guilt over past deceptions one is likely to feel. Gay clients are little comforted by being told that if parents, siblings, and intimate friends really love them these people will eventually accept the clients' gay identities. The problem for the clients is not only testing how real and deep the love of their significant others is but also needing and wanting that love and yet feeling the additional demand for a gay self-image and life-style.

Counselors should bear in mind that rejection is very possible. It would be inappropriate to minimize it or to avoid dealing with it openly and directly. The probability of at least some rejection is almost certain. Nevertheless, gays are often surprised at the acceptance they receive from significant others who are not gay. Because of the great anxiety that is experienced over the problem of coming out to significant others, the therapist may need to introduce and pursue the issue. Even when clients introduce the topic, they may only express their fear. Discussion should be guided to cover the following sequence of questions:

1.   How firmly do I accept my gay identity?
2.   What is the importance of sharing my gay identity with this person?

3.   What are apt to be the personal costs if I choose nondisclosure?
4.   What is the probability of rejection?
5.   Why do I think this is the probability?
6.   Is the rejection apt to be temporary or permanent?
7.   If I am rejected, how do I plan to handle the feelings and loss of
      the relationship?

Self-disclosure must be motivated by a positive, strong, and integrated gay identity and not by a sense of guilt over past deceptions. Self-disclosure based upon the latter motive may cause an increase in the sense of guilt if rejection occurs and lead to social isolation and self-hatred. For this reason, the first question is intended to assess and reinforce the degree of positive self-image a gay person has. It is also valuable to stress to the gay person that if rejection happens, the problem is not the gay identity, but the significant other's inability to accept it. The client should not blame self for the other person's inadequacies. Another problem relates to former negative feelings about self. One of the rationalizations for remaining in the closet is the generalization that all heterosexuals despise gayness and are therefore rejecting. For this reason, it is important that clients look at just how real their expectations of rejection are. The facilitator should encourage the individual to consider the basis for this relationship now. Particularly, what did the significant other find in the gay person that contributed to interaction in the past? Can the gay person give any reason why knowledge of the gay identity will overshadow these qualities?

Unfortunately, self-disclosure is not advisable in all relationships. For example, Marsha and Polly told the group that they had been partners since they were young girls. Very recently, they had both been surprised and pleased when Marsha's older brother informed them that he not only realized the special nature of their relationship but approved of it as well. The fact that he was aware that they were lesbians caused them to wonder if other members of their families knew or suspected as well. They thought that they should tell everyone so they would not have to worry about it.

This plan sounded reasonable at first hearing, but when the group found out that the young women still lived with their families and depended upon them financially, some members had doubts. Then Marsha added that her father was an alcoholic who frequently physically abused members of the family. He had also made very derisive comments about "queers" on a number of occasions. Under these circumstances, any positive results from their revelation were unlikely, and, in fact, there might be real danger.

At the same time, gay persons who are living in a destructive manner have no right to expect approval of their behavior, especially if their motives for coming out are destructive. The assertion of gay identity is sometimes used to punish people who are believed to have inflicted pain in the past. Clients who seem to need to get even must understand that destructive motives lead to destructive behavior, and that through such behavior they, too, will be hurt. Under such circumstances, rejection by the significant other is almost certain.

In all cases when self-disclosure is being considered, the client should ask, "Is knowledge of my gay identity important to the continuance and growth of this particular relationship?" If it is important, the motives are positive, and the client is sufficiently secure in his or her gay identity, then self-disclosure would seem warranted. Preparing for this act in the group can be very helpful. The facilitator should encourage individuals to discuss how they plan to make the disclosures and what reactions they anticipate. Role playing and particularly reverse role playing often bring new insights. Alternative scripts of the interaction based on different reactions as well as the probable reaction can be explored.

Rejection may very well occur, but unless internal or interpersonal dynamics definitely mitigate against coming out, risks in coming out to others are necessary to incorporate the gay identity within the relationships. In fact, to avoid doing so may have negative effects, as the following situation points out.

Liz was a member of a self-awareness group and was discussing her relationship with her mother. Liz had come to grips with her identity and was quite comfortable with her gay relationships, but she had been noticing significant changes in what had always been a warm relationship with her mother. They no longer had any eye contact or enjoyed doing things together; they seemed to be drifting apart. Liz had figured that her mother might be getting senile. Subsequent discussion brought out, much to Liz's surprise, that she was projecting the entire responsibility for distancing onto her mother. She then realized that by hiding her relationship with Ann from her mother, she had shut out much of her life from her mother as well. This concerned her so greatly that she had to explore the need to tell her mother about her lesbian relationship. In the next group session,

Liz was all smiles as she described the delightful rapprochement with her mother.

If one's worst fears come true in disclosure, the support of the group will often prove exceedingly important. The rejection will elicit help through the grieving process and afterwards as the client adjusts to the new circumstances. The facilitator may need to insist upon this group activity, since the felt pain of other group members may cause them to avoid processing of the pain and reawakened guilt about being gay.

In coming out to parents and other important people, an even more subtle problem can be the client's expectation of total acceptance. Some internal conflicts or guilt over nondisclosure are likely to arise from the feeling that love from parents, siblings, and other intimates has been unconditional. However, despite the guilt, an unconscious expectation frequently exists that acceptance of the gay identity will also be unconditional. As a result, gay clients may be frustrated and disappointed when they receive conditional acceptance, such as, "I love and I will always love you, even though you're gay." In such cases, it is necessary to focus on the perspectives of the significant others. Clients should remember that these people are likely to have a different set of attitudes toward homosexual behavior and a gay life-style. Those attitudes that are oppressive to gays frequently are confirming attitudes for many heterosexuals to whom acceptance and approval of a gay life-style are very different matters.

Not infrequently, a continuing, perhaps even fatalistic, acceptance is the most that the heterosexual can give at first. Gays should see acceptance as the basis for eventual approval. With the help of the gay person, the significant other may be able to overcome negative stereotypes and adjust his or her personal attitudes towards gays. Clients who complain that taking on a helping role is unfair should be reminded that, as gays, the road to self-acceptance has probably taken considerable time and energy; to expect something different from significant others is not realistic. Gays will need much love and patience to help the ones that they love to develop understanding.

In a group session, Harry expressed a good deal of resentment toward Bob and Alice. The couple had been very close friends of his for a number of years. In fact, they had been two of the first people to whom he had asserted his gay identity. Their acceptance and support since then had meant a great deal to him. Recently Harry had met Clancy and became very intimate. At Bob and Alice's suggestion, Harry brought Clancy to a small party given by the friends. Although everyone present knew Harry was gay, they virtually ignored Clancy. Both men left the party hurt and angry, feeling that Clancy had been deliberately snubbed. When Harry confronted his friends about this a few days later, they were surprised. They told Harry that what had happened was certainly not intentional and that they hoped that they could somehow make it up to Clancy as well as Harry. Harry told the group that he never intended to bring a gay friend to Bob and Alice's again. The other group members felt that Harry's attitude was unfair, because Bob and Alice had accepted Harry's gay life-style from the beginning. Now they were dealing with a new dimension of it, and Harry should give them a chance to understand his relationship with Clancy.

Introducing a lover to significant others brings up the issue of homoerotic feelings and behaviors. Harry and Clancy obviously did more than just smile at each other in their relationship. Residual discomfort concerning homosexual behavior may lead to some social blunders among people who have come to terms with the gay identity of a friend. Gays may complain, and rightly so, that a gay love relationship is much more than just going to bed together, but it may take time for nongays to realize this. Gloria expressed it this way: "Mom and Dad were never really able to accept the fact that I'm a lesbian until they really got to know Polly [her partner], but now they treat her like part of the family. They are always telling her to see to it that I do this or that or the other thing. Sure it took a while to accept Polly, but now they expect us to be together. They really got upset when we almost split up a while back."

Having made the decision to come out leads to the question of how to assert a gay identity. Gay clients should realize that no pat formula exists for coming out to others. Again, role playing the disclosure in group meetings prior to the actual event has often proved helpful. Anxiety about coming out to someone very important can prompt what might be called the hit-and-run technique, such as a letter, a telephone call, or a casual remark at a party. These methods are decidedly inappropriate. The gay person's presence allows for both privacy and time for response. It is vitally important that significant others have the opportunity to process the new reality as much as necessary. Even allowing for this, gay persons must always remember that, despite their very best efforts, hurt, confusion, and even anger may follow. The significant others must now begin the process of acceptance, which has probably taken the gay person much time. Therefore, talking the subject to death in one session may be more of a hindrance than a help. Questions should certainly be answered forthrightly but frequently the most eloquent proof to others of the appropriateness of a gay life-style is the positive and self-actualizing effects of the gay person's actions.

If the gay person's identity is really important to the quality of the relationship, then, in general, the appropriate time to make that identity known is the present. Many gays have stated that the best time to come out is when discussion naturally leads up to it rather than making a "great announcement." When one's gay identity gives particular value to the gay person's point of view in a discussion, then identifying oneself as gay is appropriate. However, the gay person must be ready to spend time helping the listeners to process the information.

6

Understanding the Special Problems of Youth

Although the material in previous chapters applies equally to gay youths, it brings up some special issues. Sexual matters of children and adolescents remain particularly sensitive in our society. As Clark (1977) points out, we are products of a sex-denying culture. The ideal, despite all evidence to the contrary, is that youths will abstain from sexual activity until marriage and have no need to consider their sexual identity.

The difficulties from suppressing sexual discussion are greatly multiplied for gay youths. The homophobic adult population denies the possibility of gayness among the young. If gay youths fail to cope with this situation, social forces work to eradicate their sexuality. The youth's self-identity becomes inconsequential in the face of the adult need to avoid facts.

71

The fact remains, however, that young people do experiment sexually. A significant number of boys and girls under age sixteen (Kinsey and others, 1948, 1953) experiment with homosexual behavior which remains the choice of some in later years. There is no scientific evidence that particular experiences produce homosexuals, but homosexual experiences do confirm homoerotic feelings just as heterosexual experiences confirm heteroerotic feelings. Denial or avoidance of their homosexuality only isolates the homoerotically oriented youth and can inhibit the emergence of a positive gay identity.

Developmental Issues

Development of a sexual identity should be an integral part of overall personality growth. Although some awareness of gender preference may exist even prior to grammar school ("Removing the Stigma," 1977; Bell and Weinberg, 1978), erotic feelings are most likely to become prominent during adolescence, when sexual role testing is critical (Morin and Schultz, 1978). Heteroerotic feelings find both societal and peer confirmation, although actual sexual experimentation may be discouraged. Social institutions assume heterosexuality, and young people of both sexes can talk about heterosexual crushes with their peers. The heterosexual youth has ample opportunity to test his or her sexual-affectional identity and confirm sexual feelings. The story is radically and sadly different for the homoerotically oriented youth. Many adult gays look back on their adolescent years as an agonizing period of development and a time of emotional or social isolation.

The presenting problem among children that is often brought to the counselor is a crisis precipitated by discovery of homosexual experimentation. Adults are more likely to consider sex play significant than are children and they are likely to describe such activity among same-sex peers as homosexual. The adults may label the children as "queer" on the basis of one incident and then exacerbate the problem by expressing disgust, anger, and hurt. By the time parents and children arrive at the counselor's office, the demand is likely to be "Our child is queer. Fix her."

The counselor must first deal with the crisis event, and the parents should be the immediate point of intervention. The counselor should see the parents and child separately, since the parents could create even more trauma for the child. Meanwhile, the child must be engaged in an inter-personal activity during the first parent conference during which feelings of being liked are communicated by agency personnel. An arm around the shoulder can convey the important message that the child is not loath-some. After the parents have expressed their feelings, the counselor should determine what events have occurred since the discovery. Because the parents are likely to be focused on the homosexual act, they will need to be reassured that this will be dealt with, but first it is essential to know how the discovery has affected subsequent parent-child interaction. Diffusing the crisis requires bringing the relationship back to the usual interactional patterns; to do this, past as well as present family functioning must be assessed. The counselor should carefully avoid interjections in-tended to correct or educate the parents during this time.

After establishing prior and current interactional patterns, the counselor can take an educative role. The parents should understand that homosexual behavior, particularly in the preadolescent years, is not con-firmation that the child is gay. No special significance should be placed on the act. Sexual experimentation does not involve the same social implica-tions, motivation, or significance for children that it does for adults. The parents should understand that a continued negative focus on the event may only cause the child to believe he or she is bad. Preteen children are very prone to accept what their parents say as being absolute and true. If parents consider their child sick, evil, or queer, the child is likely to accept their judgments unquestioningly and internalize them.

After the counselor and parents have worked to put the sexual behavior into perspective, the parents may want to forget the whole matter. The counselor should point out that such an approach will not answer the needs of the child or family, since the events have affected everyone. Intervention is intended to help each family member return to patterns that are natural, consistent with past words and actions, and conducive to self-actualization. Loving and reassuring words will only have temporary value if parents and others are acting and feeling negatively or are still reacting to the crisis. It is important that the same-sex parent be helped to show affection, particularly if this has been usual in the past. Parents should permit close same-sex friendships, including with playmates involved in the sexual experimentation, and should not dis-courage signs of physical affection in these relationships. If other parents are aware of and involved in what has happened, the family should be asked to involve them in the process just described. If siblings are also aware, they will also need to be included in the interventive process.

At this point the child should be seen. It is advisable to discuss general sexuality and not focus on the homosexual nature of the child's behavior. Two points should be made in these counseling sessions. The first is that sex is not a bad thing but something that parents see as belonging to the adult world. The second point is that the parents may have said many things that hurt the child because they were upset but that they love their child as much as always. In interviews and at home, the parents should show this love and reassurance in a warm, unconditional, and physical way. The child needs to *feel* the security and love that he or she may believe is lost. While the presence of the counselor during family interactions may offer reassurance and support, the parents should take the initiative because the child is concerned with them.

With the onset of puberty, the issue of identity becomes critical for the gay youth. General feelings about being different become more sexual, and relations with friends of the same sex become eroticized. Pejorative labels such as "queer," "fag," "homo," "fairy," or "dyke" become common. At some point during the teens, homoerotic feelings and sexual identity may be explored through questioning or through sexual behavior, because adolescence is, by its nature, a time of hypothesizing about and testing identity (Erikson, 1968). As with younger children, parents and counselors should not assign more meaning or significance to homosexual behavior at this point than the actors place upon it. Homosexual experimentation (as well as heterosexual experimentation) continues into adolescence, and although it is more significant than during childhood, it is not necessarily an indication of a homosexual identity. Kinsey and others (1948) point out that before the age of sixteen, 60 percent of the males that they interviewed had engaged in some form of homosexual behavior, and for 25 percent this behavior occurred incidentally on more than a few occasions. However, the generally accepted figure is that homosexuals comprise approximately 10 percent of the population. These figures indicate the need to use extreme caution in labeling anyone as homosexual just because of homosexual activity.

Nevertheless, in at least 10 percent of the youths, homosexual behavior is not a passing phase. The particular attitudes of the youth toward same-sex relationships must be assessed. Exploration should be based upon the youth's needs and not upon some arbitrary "appropriate age." Dank (1971) indicates that of his male homosexual sample, 15 percent self-identified between the ages of ten and fourteen, and 79 percent between the ages of fifteen and nineteen. Jay and Young (1979) report that according to responses to the question "At what age did you first realize you were a homosexual or gay or sexually different?", 75 percent of the males were self-aware by age nineteen. The breakdown by ages was: nine to twelve, 31 percent; thirteen to fifteen, 29 percent; and sixteen to nineteen, 16 percent. The same study indicates that girls and women identified as lesbian at a later age: 57 percent by age nineteen and 20 percent between the ages of twenty and twenty-four. Woodman (1979), in her research with 200 gay women, found that 20 percent had accepted a gay identity by age nineteen. A significant number had been aware of their gayness to some degree in childhood or adolescence but denied or repressed this fact for as many as thirty years. Quite likely, many more gay men and women would self-identify before adulthood if support were more available (Woodman, 1979).

But what is that realized identity to mean? Homosexual youths have almost no nonjudgmental resources from which to seek an answer to this question. Repeatedly, gay clients have stated that when they either suspected or became convinced of their homosexual identity, they felt a need to find out more about the subject but felt they had nowhere to turn. Cautious testing of adult attitudes indicated extreme danger of rejection. Most peer attitudes were hostile and involved the same stereotypes already known to the client.

Tammy, aged seventeen, was referred to family service by her supervisor after she had, with much trepidation, expressed her love for Ms. Blair. When Ms. Blair indicated that Tammy's feelings were not reciprocated and that she should seek help because her feelings were sick, Tammy broke down, saying, "This always happens to me." However, Ms. Blair did make a referral for counseling. The social worker explored identity issues with Tammy and learned that the young woman had known from her early teens that her feelings for other girls were frequently stronger than those of friendship. She had told this to her best friend Laurie, who told all the other girls in their clique to stay away from Tammy because she was a "bull dyke." Tammy felt that Ms. Blair was a warm, understanding person, yet Ms. Blair recoiled with repugnance and rejection.

The impact of negative stereotypes has been described previously. However, it is important to stress the effect they may have on the adolescent's self-concept. If the only information available is negative, it can have devastating consequences. Usually there is strong pressure on adolescents to conform in such areas as dress, life goals, and dating. The combination of little available information, homophobia, and stereotypes creates a number of dilemmas for youth dealing with homoerotic feelings, preferences, and activity. For the gay youth, as for the gay adult, to say, "Yes, I am," is not sufficient. Behavior must reinforce acknowledgment. Differences in self-expression depend on the responses of other individuals. Social situations for the adult gay are likely to be closed to the adolescent due to legal restrictions. For example, Tom, age fourteen, appeared one evening at a meeting of the university gay activists. He was excited about finally meeting other gays and requested permission to participate in the meeting. The organization members referred Tom to churches that had teenage gay groups, but at the next meeting they discussed about what to do to protect the organization from community and university censure if other young teens showed up.

The degree to which the youth's identity as gay has been discovered or asserted to others is important to the counseling. The client's sexual-affectional preference may be known only to the client; the client may have disclosed it to a few friends; or family, peers, and other people may know. For example, John, a sixteen-year-old, stated that several gay and heterosexual peers knew he was gay, but he lived in constant fear that his identity would be discovered by his parents. Groups of gay teenagers within school settings appear to be on the rise. School counselors and sex educators indicate that more students are identifying themselves as gay and seeking help in understanding their preference. Nevertheless, most youths still fear helping professionals. Although self-chosen peer contacts may seem safe, knowledge by adults carries the threat of labeling and exposure beyond the boundaries desired by the young person. Counselors have usually not explicated their nonjudgmental attitudes toward a gay life-style or their willingness for self-actualizing interaction with youths who are concerned about a homosexual identity. Because of the legal status of a teenager and fears of exposure, any youth who seeks out a counselor to discuss gayness has likely done a great deal of soul searching first. The level of pain that accompanies coming out and seeking help should not be exacerbated; rather, it should be alleviated through acceptance and sympathetic counseling.

The nature of intervention depends on whether the parents know that the adolescent is gay. Because of social and legal matters and the heightened emotionality related to youth and sexuality, great care must be exercised. It is extremely important to be aware of the young person's rights to confidentiality and treatment and related legalities. The youth who is seeking ongoing counseling should be informed of legal limitations so that ways of responding to them can be discussed and agreed upon.

At the beginning of the counseling relationship, gay adolescents may protect themselves by making oblique references and questions, such as "I know this queer guy. Should I have anything to do with him? Why is everybody mean to him? Is he sick?" The variations are endless. Counselors should restrain the urge to obtain specifics and focus instead on the two basic needs underlying such an approach: information and reassurance. Any vagueness by the client should be allowed to stand, since any inquiries that might be interpreted as seeking verification about the subject of discussion will probably elicit a strategic and hasty retreat. Answer the youth's questions simply, directly, and with an accepting demeanor.

Knowledge is the important goal of the interaction. Since the young person has little information, a simple question such as "Is he sick?" provides an opportunity to give plenty of data concerning same-sex preference and a gay life-style. The counselor can encourage the client to ask other questions about what the counselor is saying and thus increase the educational value of the interview. Throughout the interaction, the counselor should reinforce the fact that the friend simply has different sexual-affectional needs than do most of the client's other peers. This individual can still be different and yet be happy and have a good life.

The counselor should leave the door open for further contact by still referring to the friend. For example, the counselor can say, "Tell your friend that if he wants to talk about his feelings, I'd be happy to do so. Certainly, if you have any further questions that will help you to understand your friend, I'd be glad to talk more with you." It is extremely important that the adolescent leave with the feeling that the counselor accepts homosexual feelings and likes gay persons.

However, providing information as needed is not ideal, because most gay adolescents will not approach an adult for help. Information concerning sexuality, homosexuality, and a gay life-style should be made available to all young persons. Morin and Schultz (1978, pp. 144-145) give the three following principles:

> Children must be informed of the existence of gay-identified adults and of gay life-styles.
> Positive models of gay-identified adults must be available to children . . . . Sex education classes are a good place to begin presenting young people positive models of gay life-styles.
> Opportunities for exploration of gay feelings and life-styles must be available in a context which neither discourages experimentation nor promotes any particular development outcome.

Identity Confusion or Crisis

Incidental participation in homosexual behavior may create an identity crisis or at least concern, triggering a search for help. For a younger adolescent, do *not* automatically assume sexual interaction. Peers may be responsible for mislabeling nonsexual behavior, such as effeminate behavior in boys, masculine behavior in girls, or activities that are unacceptable to peers because they do not fit teenage, heterosexist stereotypes. To avoid mislabeling, the counselor must clarify the meanings of all words and make clear, in a nonjudgmental manner, just what being gay is and is not.

The young person may approach a counselor with a question such as "Something happened between John and me and I liked it. Does that mean I'm queer?" If what actually happened was some form of homosexual behavior, the significance that the client gives to the interaction must be determined. Particular care should be taken to maintain the client's frame of reference. Every effort should be made to avoid hasty labeling. This point is especially important with regard to adolescents, who may hold rigidly to stereotypes. Not infrequently, young persons can believe that since they performed a homosexual act, they are homosexual. To complicate the picture even further, the line that separates heterosexual from homosexual may shift at different stages of adolescence. For example, mutual masturbation may not be labeled deviant at thirteen but may be at fifteen. The counseling should therefore help the young client to put incidents of homosexual behavior into perspective.

Four points need to be considered in the interaction:

1. Homosexual and heterosexual experimentation is not unusual among young people.
2. The fact that a young person finds pleasure in a homosexual act is not necessarily an indication of homosexuality.
3. The type of sexual activity actually engaged in should not be seen as confirmation of sexual orientation.
4. Adolescence is a time for discovering more about oneself sexually as well as in many other ways. There is no need to establish one's identity or to accept a label used by others unless the person feels that it fits with the self-image.

Sexual orientation is usually decided over a period of time as primary sexual-affectional feelings are understood and as a life-style that is appropriate to those feelings is developed.

During discussion of evolving identity, the counselor should take great care not to imply that he or she wishes to avoid or delay the need to come to terms with a perceived or suspected gay identity. Sexual-affectional identity may be established at any age. Projecting an attitude that such a decision should be postponed until adulthood may freeze the youthful client in the problem situation. It is destructive when counselors, due to their own discomfort, choose to avoid discussing the youthful client's needs and therefore retard the efforts of the young person to develop a positive, healthy sexual identity and life-style. Additionally, given the prevalent misinformation concerning homosexuality, therapeutic avoidance may increase a sense of negative self-worth and even lead to self-destructive behavior.

Because of such reluctance by therapists, many clients may need to retrace many of their developmental steps when they become young adults. They have to cope with various issues that should have been resolved during their adolescent years. Also, they must undo the harmful effects of adolescent isolation and groping with issues related to their gay sexual-affectional identity.

The young person who has self-identified as gay may ask, "I'm gay, what should I do?" The counselor should first ascertain whether the homosexual identity itself or its implications pose the true problem.

If the problem is identity crisis, it must be dealt with forthrightly.

The impulsive behavior that is characteristic of adolescents makes the crisis potentially more dangerous than it is for adults. Kindly assurances that this feeling is probably only a stage or that the client's possible gayness is not of concern at present are definitely inappropriate. A disconcertingly high percentage of gay people have either contemplated or actually attempted suicide while first experiencing their adolescent identity crisis.

Of particular concern is the parents. If they have become aware that their child is gay, they should be a part of the crisis resolution, especially if their attitudes are negative and are therefore contributing to the client's distress. If the parents are unaware that their child is gay, the counselor should remember that bluntly revealing a homosexual identity is likely to cause emotional strain between the youth and the parents at best or a major family crisis at worst. In any event, revealing the youth's gayness is unethical and/or dangerous for the young client. If the parents must approve continued therapeutic intervention, it is suggested that their consent first be obtained under the rubric of "adolescent adjustment problems." Parents should be carefully instructed about the therapeutic importance of respecting the privacy of their son's or daughter's interaction with the counselor. Their natural desire to know what the problem is must be tempered by the child's need for confidentiality.

As the young person begins to come to terms with his or her gay sexual-affectional identity, the issue of sharing that awareness can and should be considered. Making a mutual decision will require that the general quality of the relationship between the young person and the parents be considered. Coming out at home is a crucial decision that risks the loss of basic human needs on which the young person depends. For example, Jon, age nineteen, related to a group meeting one evening that after his family learned he was homosexual, older siblings beat him; he was then thrown out of the house for disrupting the family. He was forced to live for several years on the streets of a major urban area.

The decision to divulge a gay sexual identity to one's parents must take into consideration several factors besides those discussed in Chapter Five. These include:

1.   How comfortable the client is with his or her identity
2.   How flexible and egalitarian the youth-parent interaction is
3.   The capacity of the parents to deal with their child's identity
4.   The parents' ability to respect the adolescent's capacity to know that he or she is gay.

Protests by the youth that coming out to parents will lead to rejection must not be unquestioned. Nevertheless, the youthful client's confidence must be honored, and his or her decision must be respected. The young person must understand, though, that ongoing help will require some kind of contact with the parents.

In preliminary interviews with parents, discussion can be about the general area of adolescent development rather than sexual identity. Hopefully these discussions will help the counselor to understand the relationships in the family. Following interviews with the parents, a joint parent-child session should be held in which issues of relationship, adolescent needs, and parental attitudes can be explored. Almost every family has areas of disagreement. As the family discusses how these are handled, they and the counselor can assess communication, respect, openness to new ideas, and family values. Positive interaction can pave the way for dealing with the young person's gayness.

After working with parents and child, follow-up interview with the young person is helpful so that the youth and the counselor can assess parental attitudes and establish further goals for counseling. If both believe that the risks of disclosure are minimal and that potential benefits to the young client outweigh the benefits of nondisclosure, the counselor should inform the parents in a follow-up conference. Coming out is likely to arouse intense negative reactions from the parents, and they will need an opportunity to ventilate their feelings. It is not advisable for the youth to bear the brunt of initial responses. The counselor's role is to help the parents work through these feelings, to provide sympathy, and not to take sides. Subsequent interaction with the parents should combine educative counseling with exploring ways to handle the child's gayness within the family.

Before the follow-up conference with the parents, the youth and the counselor should review possible parental reactions and ideas for how the youth will respond to parents. At this point, intervention will probably focus on the effects of disclosure on the parent-youth relationship and assisting the parents and child to make appropriate adjustments. During this period the counselor must sympathize with and help the young gay person to understand that the parents will need time to adjust.

Fairchild and Hayward (1979), parents of gay children and leaders in the Parents of Gays Organization, offer good advice. They suggest that parents should try to help themselves and their gay child. Fairchild and Hayward recommend three main ways for parents to help themselves.

First, parents can dispel feelings of isolation by meeting other parents of gay children. The counselor may help in this regard. Second, parents can meet gay men and women and unlearn negative stereotypes. Gay organizations can help here. Finally, parents should learn about gayness. The counselor might offer parents a reading program and offer opportunities to discuss their feelings and questions.

To help their gay child, parents should offer love, openness, and trust. First, they should be aware of the attitude that they project toward their son or daughter. For example, parents should avoid using "them" or "those people" when referring to homosexuals and instead use positive terms such as *gays* and *lesbians*. Second, parents should avoid establishing new, restrictive regulations. Although the intent may be to protect the young person from bad influences, it is more likely to convey distrust and discomfort. Parents should welcome their child's gay friends into the family's social interactions, especially the child's closest friend. Gay adolescents, like their heterosexual counterparts, may go steady, and parents should be accepting and permit signs of affection. Finally, Fairchild and Hayward make a crucial point regarding friendships with older gays. Long-held fears about "homosexual recruitment" may cause parents to presume the worst when their child has an older gay friend. In fact, older gays have a strong desire to help younger gays develop sound, positive identities. Relating to stable, mature gay adults can help the gay adolescent develop a healthy sexual-affectional self-identity.

If the gay young person's identity is already known by the parents, the presenting question of "What should I do?" may indicate either crisis or severe strain in the parent-child relationship. In a crisis stemming from the adolescent's identity, intervention must first be directed to stabilizing the family situation and helping the young person regain feelings of security and self-worth. The client's parents can then move toward accepting the young person. The counselor, client, and family will assess whether the crisis is simply the rupture in family relationships caused by the knowledge of the child's self-perceived identity or a re-emerging identity crisis for the gay adolescent. If an identity crisis has reappeared, the parent-child relationships must still be stabilized. Simultaneously, attention should be given to resolving the young person's identity issues, as described in Chapter Three. However, unlike adult identity conflicts, the effect of significant others upon the therapeutic effort must also be considered. Although parents may be encouraged to relax and sympathize with their child during identity clarification, their ongoing concerns will still manifest within the family. Both parents and the child should be encouraged to voice these concerns as they arise, preferably in joint interviews.

The counselor will need to assume a strong, ongoing educative role with both the youth and the parents. Very likely, destructive and alienating feelings that arise will be traceable to stereotypes about homosexuality. Without adequate knowledge, hostile attitudes toward the youth's gay identity will prevent the family from reestablishing a supportive, growth-stimulating environment. The counselor should be especially sensitive to attitudinal regression in the parents. Even if parents initially accept their child's gayness, they often become more troubled as the reality becomes more evident and as they begin to associate their child with the negative stereotypes. These regressive feelings may give rise to the following questions and comments: "How will my child's sexual preference affect our lives?" "Perhaps the whole thing is just a passing phase." "Life will be terrible for him." "Maybe, since the child is young, she can be changed." "My child is just too young to make such decisions. I'll have to take this matter into my own hands."

Whether a panic reaction is immediate or delayed, young persons are essentially helpless when confronted by unaccepting parents. When such parents seek counseling with the intent of curing their child, several dynamics are apparent. First, there is crisis within the family, in which the adolescent's sense of self is denied. The youth is considered unable to make such a self-identification. If the youth insists upon his or her self-identity, parents seek to invalidate it, perhaps by projecting the blame upon some seducer. The only appropriate course of action from the parents' view is to stamp out the homosexuality. Ironically, the sexual reality is at once denied and yet affirmed by the desire to seek therapy.

Having been caught in this confusion, the young person may be forced to resolve a variety of issues. The parents' previous openness and acceptance and their desire to explore the child's sexual identity in an open, nonjudgmental manner are replaced by demands that the young person accept the goals of the parents, who insist that they know what's best. Young gays in this position quickly learn that their own sense of identity or their desired therapeutic goals are lost to parental needs and expectations. Open insistence on a gay identity is likely to increase the crisis and prolong the conflict. The only way out for the adolescent may be to obey the parents. John, during a group discussion, laughed cynically: "What do you mean 'no cure'—I was 'cured' three times when I was a kid!" He explained that to satisfy parental expectations and to avoid therapy that he did not desire, he would proclaim that he no longer desired sex with other boys. His parents would then withdraw him from therapy until he "relapsed," when they would return him to therapy.

A panic reaction—the parental desire for change and the youth's outward compliance—may be evidenced by a sudden decision to discontinue the counseling. Explanations may be vague and evasive, or there may be angry charges of making or letting the child become a homosexual. The best steps here are preventative and should begin with the first interactions with the parents, when roles in the therapeutic effort are being established. Intensive educating about homosexuality and the gay life-style for the parents should be a main part of the total therapeutic effort. Second, sessions with the parents should be planned regularly so that their fears, concerns, self-blame, and questions can be acted on. Without continued parental involvement, it may be impossible to calm panicked parents who decide to terminate counseling.

Unfortunately, it may be unwise or even destructive for some gay youths to reveal their identity to their parents when they seek counseling. The parents may be unyielding homophobes or have poor interactions with the child. Overly authoritarian parents may not respect the young person's ability to understand or develop valid self-perceptions of identity. Such attitudes will be verified in the early interviews. With such parents, the counselor should broaden the counseling to consider adolescent development problems. Under this framework, issues concerning sexual identity can be explored along with other developmental issues but in a manner that will not be viewed as sexual-identity counseling. This will allow the youth to discuss a gay life-style with the counselor without threatening the parents. Helping the parents and adolescent to discuss neutral topics such as vocational goals may help them to establish continuous contact. Also, the youth can learn to generalize experiences related to supportive and oppressive systems.

The Adolescent Gay in an Adolescent World

Gay teenagers, like gay adults, are very likely to face social stress that may require counseling. In fact, some peers are quite likely to have severe negative reactions because they have not firmly established their own sexual identity and easily panic at the thought of homoerotic feelings. This fact, plus the prevailing myth that homosexuality is sick or evil, can cause a gay youth to have a number of destructive peer interactions. The more similar the heterosexual or identity-conflicted youth and the known gay peer are, the more threatening an interaction between them will be to the former. Also, the more the gay youth can be made to conform to stereotypes, the greater the social and emotional distance between heterosexual and homosexual adolescents will be. Gay youths are socially required to be sufficiently different so that other youths are not threatened and yet not too different so that they can be somewhat accepted. Therefore, in trying to establish a gay self-identity, teenagers may find that they have entered almost unwittingly into conflicting interactional situations for which they have few coping skills. Negative experiences are likely to be severe and direct.

Chuck spoke of having his first homosexual experience at age ten with a neighbor boy who was four years older. Pleased both by the sexual encounter and the attention from the older boy, whom he very much admired, he actively pursued other sexual interactions. Soon other boys were seeking him out for sexual favors, which he was happy to provide. Thus, a pattern of behavior was formed that continued through Chuck's adolescence. He joked about having been "Chuck the willing and available neighborhood fairy." Chuck entered counseling in his twenties, complaining of his inability to maintain a relationship. The counselor inquired whether his past experiences may have been the cause of his problem. Chuck didn't think so. "Oh, the guys kidded me about being queer, but they never really hassled me." When asked what he and these friends did, Chuck responded, "Have sex, what else?" Further discussion brought out that Chuck's interaction with his peers was almost totally restricted to sex. By being a willing sexual object, Chuck had come to define himself and his interactions primarily in those terms, expecting that this was all that any gay partner wanted. As a result, in any relationship, Chuck's efforts were almost totally focused on making himself desirable. When the intensity of the sex lessened, he always took it as a sign of rejection. This in turn triggered arguments and eventual breakups.

The gay adolescent may believe that being gay means, in part, behaving in stereotypical ways. This belief may arise from a lack of knowledge of the diversity of a gay life-style. The young person simply adopts those behaviors that he assumes are a part of being homosexual. The need for some niche in the adolescent social world may cause the young gay to behave outrageously, particularly if other known gay adolescents act this way. Thus, counseling should teach the young gay the diversity of a gay life-style and refute the myths about homosexuals.

Gay youths must know that they have the right to define their identity in a way that is self-actualizing. The counselor should go over with adolescents social and personal activities that have been satisfying and meaningful and then discuss how to continue those activities as a gay person. In many instances, the youth will understand that being gay is irrelevant to pursuing and finding satisfaction in particular vocations and interests. Gay youths should be encouraged to explore whatever interests they have with adults who provide leadership in those areas. This may demand advocacy and educational efforts by the counselor if the youth's gay identity creates discomfort for the adult leaders.

In dealing with clients who adopt stereotypical behavior in response to peer pressure, the counselor should not underestimate the force of this pressure. What the young person must understand is that while fulfilling such expectations may seem expedient, the long-range effects can be very self-destructive. The meaning and effect of stereotypes should be explored when young people are acting them out.

During a group discussion, Ann and Ruth were complaining about the verbal abuse they experienced at school after their lesbian relationship had become known. After some extended discussion about how to respond to the situation, Tom laughed and said he didn't see what all the fuss was about. Everybody at school knew that he was gay, and he had few problems. The group was surprised and curious about how Tom gained acceptance from his classmates. "I just give them what they want," he chuckled, "You'd be surprised at how much quieter they are after they've asked me to take care of them." "Bullshit!" interjected Alan, "I tried that route. The guy seemed real satisfied when we were parked alone in the car but him and his buddies beat the crap out of me the next day." Ann added heatedly, "And besides, Tom, the other girls are just nasty. They don't want sex with us but the *boys* do. They keep saying that all we need is a good screw to set us straight. And they mean it!"

An extended discussion of the effects of peer knowledge of one's gay identity ensued. The girls had to deal with the threat of rape and giving into demands to become demeaned sex objects. Alan's incident generated discussion of the dynamics that may be at work when acceding to the sexual advances of peers who are either unaccepting of one's gay identity or confused about their own sexual-affectional preference. In such cases, the other person might react violently if the experience is satisfying. Tom was asked what he got out of such sexual escapades. He responded that he really didn't mind and he received pleasure. When asked about how his contacts felt about him, he shrugged the question off as being of no consequence. This response led to an extended and heated interchange about whether it did matter, how the others saw this behavior affecting him, and the effects on his self-image.

Young gays should recognize when the expectations and demands of peers are self-destructive. In some instances, this may mean that one's gay identity should not be asserted if self-assertion is irrelevent to the situation or if it would lead to a destructive interaction. In other instances, it may mean withdrawal from an already destructive situation. This is not the same as denial or repression of one's gay identity, nor does it require absolute avoidance of peers.

This entire issue relates to the problem about deciding with whom to share one's gay identity. Should one's gay identity be shared at all, or is it more judicious to be quiet? In counseling with young gays, it is particularly important to deal with the relationship between sexual-affectional identity and one's broader social identity. Being gay does make a difference. If the gay identity is not known by any or most peers, the problem of its being discovered or becoming more widely known is always present. Exposure by others can cause great stress for gay youths. Therefore, they must explore this possibility and establish a plan for dealing with the situation if it arises. Pretending to be nongay may appear to be the best defensive position, but adolescents may be able to relate to the experiences of gay adults who have learned that such a strategy has heavy psychological costs. Repressing this dimension of self is made difficult by the constant need to hide real feelings. Also, social expectations become greater in later years. For example, besides dating in adolescence, engagement and marriage are expected by the time one is twenty-five. Reintegrating the sexual self after years of such defensive stratagems can be difficult and confusing. The game playing must be undone, and the whole process of finding positive circumstances for testing and validating reality must begin at a much later and less appropriate time. It is hardly ideal to enter sexual adolescence in adulthood just because it is safer then.

Retreat into social isolation is equally dysfunctional. Social inter-action is essential to the development of a healthy personal and social identity. If identity development is to progress, the gay young person must act in a way that is consistent with the sense of self. However, one's actions must consider the social situation. The counselor must help the gay youth to search out, evaluate, and use responsible opportunities for means of asserting self-identity. Such assertiveness should not allow others to determine how the gay adolescent will act. When the assertion of self-identify is deemed appropriate, significant support systems will be needed. The gay adolescent will need understanding and supportive adults with whom ongoing dilemmas of identity development and asser-tion can be discussed in depth. Counselors bear a major responsibility in this regard. Gay youth will frequently need help in finding places where they can be respected as gay persons and find a healthy, supportive, and affirming atmosphere. Finally, they will need gay peer friends with whom they can grow as self-actualizing persons.

Afterward

While preparing the material for this chapter, the authors were urged to avoid the subject completely because it was too sensitive. How-ever, both clinical experience and research data clearly show that gay adolescents do exist. The helping professionals must accept their respon-sibility in dealing with the developmental needs of these young people. Also, gay preteens and adolescents have some unique problems that must be considered in their own terms. Finally, because of both the general and the gay media, gay young people are learning they are not alone. Consequently, they are seeking alternative resources and supports appro-priate to their life-style.

7

Enhancing Interpersonal Relationships

Thus far, the authors have focused on
the problems related to coming out to self and to others. In this chapter,
we will address problems concerning the client's relationships. These
problems can be like the family and interpersonal difficulties faced by
nongays. Any individual, regardless of sexual preference, can encounter
difficulties in dealing with intimate others and peers. For example, most
couples frequently have conflicts in dealing with the decisions faced in
relationships dealing with crisis and aging, as reflected in national divorce
statistics as well as in the suffering seen by helping professionals and social
agencies (Wallerstein and Kelly, 1979). However, there frequently are
additional facets to the relationship problems of gay individuals and
couples, such as the lack of familial support, both emotionally and eco-
nomically. Financial help may be essential so that a gay couple can become
truly independent.

Gay couples are affected by statutes that make homosexuality illegal in many states. Legal problems also affect the issues of child custody, survivor's benefits, hospital visitation, and so forth. Many religious denominations and congregations that may accept homosexuality do not provide spiritual reinforcement for the self-actualization of gay family units. Certainly, few gay couples have been included in the social and spiritual activities of many churches and synagogues.

Gay couples encounter rejection and oppression, which may place stress on their relationship. Traditional support systems are often hostile and do not help gay couples adjust to life crises. They can also impede problem solving at various stages of gay relationships. Because of these problems, a gay couple seeking help may avoid going to traditional agencies or helping professionals.

Therefore, it is crucial that active outreach by professionals be accompanied by a demonstrated awareness of the problems in obtaining supports. When counseling is requested, the worker must develop trust and accept that the history of the helping professions toward gays may increase initial testing in therapy. The worker must explore the degree to which presenting problems have been compounded because of oppression in the couple's environment. Also, the worker must note if the partners are at different stages of coming out to self or to others or if they still suffer from stereotyping.

Andy and Burt came to the counselor because they were frequently fighting and feared that their eight-year relationship was about to end. The presenting problem was that they were totally cooped up at home in a new city and couldn't find any "compatible" social outlets. In the process of exploration, the counselor learned that the couple had moved to this city after Burt had to leave his previous job when his employer learned that he was gay. The disclosure occurred because the couple had been picked up by the police (along with a large group of other friends) when they left a gay rights meeting. Andy expressed considerable guilt because Burt insisted that they would not be having any problems if Andy "hadn't dragged them to a meeting with all those obvious queers." The worker could not immediately begin to help Andy and Burt discover and become part of the resources available within the community. Instead, the worker had the couple explore and deal with the realities and feelings related to the factors that contributed to the presenting problem: oppression and internalized self-hate.

Although help may be sought for many problems, four problem areas will be discussed below that represent significant crises in passage during adulthood.

Problems in Maintaining Committed Relationships

Although it might be ideal if two individuals entering an intimate relationship could anticipate and discuss the realities of daily living at the onset, more often euphoria prevails. They joyously shout, "This is it!" and deal with feelings and ideas related to mutual commitment later. Some specific problem areas will be considered, including the meaning of a homosexual orientation to the relationship, space and time, roles, inclusion of others, and needs for continued growth.

As has been indicated here and in other works (Clark, 1977; Vida, 1978), a gay identity has social, companionship, and intellectual aspects as well as sexual. However, for some gays and many heterosexuals, the sexual dimension is of particular concern. Many gays incorporate the myth of the temporary nature of gay relationships and in counseling voice their concern about whether they can make the present relationship last. Research based on respondents who frequent gay bars may indirectly reinforce this myth. A generation gap or the fact that many gay couples are still in the closet frequently prevents gays who are in the process of coming out from meeting others who have sustained commitments for decades. Furthermore, an individual may have reached the point of wanting a commitment after a series of short-lived affairs. Also, examples of unstable or promiscuous heterosexual relationships may add to a client's uncertainty as may the lack of external supports.

Misinterpretation of popular movements and literature, such as O'Neill and O'Neill's *Open Marriage* (1973), sometimes leads to the advocacy of an "open nonheterosexist" sexual relationship. While both partners may agree to this, neither may have explored the ramifications. For example, allocating time to the other and time to a significant third person may require problem solving. More basic, however, is the level of trust in the commitment. Whether the relationship is exclusive or open, it may be easier to project problems onto significant others. Thus, the therapist must help each partner to deal with such issues as "Can I trust myself to remain committed?" "Can I trust another to value me as the primary person in his or her life?" "Can I trust others to recognize our commitment and not disrupt it?"

Also pertinent is clarification of what *commitment* means. Did the individuals agree to stay together for as long as they grow individually and together in this relationship for a stipulated period of time, with possible renewals of the agreement, or until death? Did both individuals agree upon a sexually exclusive relationship? Essentially, sexual trust depends on what constitutes security in a relationship.

The helping professional should not overlook the fact that in moving from romantic love to day-to-day living, expectations may change about the degree to which caring should be sexually expressed. A transition to less romantic sexual expressiveness may cause uncertainty and be misinterpreted as proving the myth that gay relationships cannot last. However, sexual problems can arise, which can have physiological, psychogenic, and social learning origins. Problems such as impotency, orgasmic dysfunction, or the inability to engage in particular sexual behaviors do require treatment. The therapist must be able to explore sexual issues. If counselors feel that such intervention is beyond their competency, referrals to knowledgeable and ethical therapists should be made. Masters and Johnson (1979) have added to the knowledge about sexual counseling with gays, and the therapist might also refer to chap. 4 in Vida's *Our Right to Love* (1978). Any referral must not coerce the client into unwanted change-in-orientation therapy or violate the client's confidentiality.

The couple may be dealing with mundane issues related to space and time needs. For instance, if any relationship is to flourish, each individual must have room to grow in self-actualizing ways. The therapist can facilitate self-actualization for the couple by helping each to explore whether various aspects of each partner are complementary or dissonant.

Jane, age twenty-six, and Becky, age thirty-five, sought counseling because their two-year relationship was on the verge of breaking up. Becky was feeling totally stifled by Jane and her friends, whose main idea of socializing was constant bar hopping. When Jane wasn't at a gay bar, she wanted Becky's undivided attention. If Jane was watching TV, Becky had to; if Jane was cooking, Becky had to at least sit in the kitchen, even if there was nothing for her to do; if Becky got on the phone, Jane got on the extension. Until last week, Becky had not said anything about feeling intellectually deprived and physically smothered. Then she erupted and told Jane, "I can't stand living like this one minute more. I've got to have some space for myself and time for cultural interests." Jane acknowledged that she should have picked up clues from Becky's increasingly late nights working and from her "sneak reading" in the bathroom. The counselor learned that Jane and Becky had enjoyed many different activities before living together, but they started out being so in love with each other that they abandoned many of them and then settled into a routine. Also, Jane thought that their relationship should be just like her parents': "They always did *everything* together, and it just proved how much they loved each other." Both partners wanted the relationship to continue and agreed to further joint interviews.

From this presenting situation, the counselor was able to begin problem solving by considering short- and long-term goals for each person as well as for Becky and Jane as a couple. Because goal setting and self-actualization demand creativity, people in relationships need time alone as well as time with significant others. The degree to which problems develop depends on how separation is interpreted by the partners as well as whether the relationship grows from some separateness in time and distance. True freedom allows for being alone or with others and returning to the intimate relationship having grown and being ready to share the new experiences.

Members of the helping professions are well aware of the need for every child, resident in an institution, and elderly person to have a place of his or her own. Partners also need places of their own. If one or both have an intense need to be inseparable, both the individuals and the relationship are in danger of suffocating. It also is not unusual for problems to arise over how the couple's home is to be kept or how its space is to be used. For example, Ludwig, age forty-five, had been a member of an alcoholism counseling group for a year before he met nineteen-year-old Mark. During that year he had stopped drinking completely. The two formed an immediate attachment, and Mark moved into Ludwig's townhouse. Six months later, the older man came to a group meeting stating that Mark was driving him back to drink: "He just has no notions of cleanliness or orderliness." The final straw came when Mark volunteered to cook dinner. "He made artichokes in my very best cookware and left the uneaten ones in the pan, which he hid in the oven where they rotted. He absolutely ruined my good pan and smelled up my kitchen." The group promptly picked up on Ludwig's constant use of *my* and insisted on exploring the meaning of this to him *and* to Mark. The counselor should be sensitive to the need to explore definitions of what is whose and how each partner moves through and within joint areas. Is there respect for the other as well as comfort and joy in sharing time and space? Is there a sense of mutual investment of time, energy, and money?

Perhaps no issues are more practical and yet more emotional than those concerning money and property. Lack of economic support can create stress in the formative years of a gay relationship, and rejection of loans by banks and family can be interpreted as reflecting the lack of worthiness of the couple as a unit. The need for economic support can also prevent coming out to others and reinforce clandestine and guilt-ridden behavior in order to meet survival needs. Also, the myth of transient gay relationships and prior experiences in which an individual has suffered financially when relationships have broken up can create fears about investing money into things for a new relationship. The worker should be alert to issues of trust and security within self and in the relationship rather than focusing totally on economics. How much a person cares for his or her partner may be reflected in the person's giving and taking. The ability to share without measuring every exchange monetarily may require increased communication between the partners about self-esteem and values in general.

Things that are important to individual learning and creativity and to the growth of the couple frequently require money. Difficulty in allocating money usually arises from basic value differences, which may reflect different sociocultural attitudes. The degree to which one feels the need for creature comforts, possessions, and cars within one's surroundings usually depends on one's socialization. Cross-cultural interaction is common in gay bars. Later, when people who have met in a bar enter a committed relationship, self-esteem issues can arise because of differences in occupational status, income, and monetary versus work contributions to the household.

Marie, who came from a very wealthy family, and Cathy had met in a dormitory at college, where the latter received social security because her working class parents were dead. When both started work and got a house, friction began to endanger their three-year relationship. Their presenting problem to the counselor was that "we need help in settling our money arguments." Cathy felt no sense of participating in making their home because Marie used money from an inheritance, while Cathy had no such reserves. Marie, in turn, was furious because Cathy "spent every last dime on more and more books, which she's always reading, and [is] not even working to help with the place." Cathy's response to this was that she felt that Marie "is using her money as an excuse to make me do the things she doesn't want to do around the house." What evolved was money as a control issue that affected role expectations in the relationship.

Counselors should be sensitive to problems related to role delineation. Gays, like their nongay peers, have been raised in a society that emphasizes role stereotyping for males and females. For heterosexual couples, socialization in families has been supported by literature and the mass media to the degree that psychological androgyny (Bem, 1975) is still more the exception than the rule. More importantly, role stereotyping is closely related to the division of tasks. For example, many individuals continue to see household chores as being feminine and car repair as being masculine, with the former tasks being less highly valued. Unfortunately, this valuation of the chores is then transferred to the person doing them. For the gay couple, physical attributes, mannerisms, interests, or aptitudes may result in one partner being designated as feminine and the other as masculine. Role stereotyping may then carry over into the total relationship. Such delineation can provide comfortable guidelines for the couple, or it can create conflict if the roles run counter to inner feelings and self-perceptions. If the therapist has stereotypical views of gays, counseling will merely reinforce such conflicts. For example, during the writing of this book, the authors heard from several mental health professionals that their colleagues frequently referred to clients as "bull dykes," "fags," or "queens" based on isolated behaviors. Such bias carries with it assumptions that preclude exploring the meanings of gayness for the person.

Conversely, to avoid previous role stereotyping, individuals may evidence reverse stereotypical task valuations that are equally strong. For example, a formerly heterosexually married person who has selected a gay life-style may reject the former role and refuse to do all jobs or chores associated with that role. For the partner, the period of establishing tasks can be tense. When conflicts do occur and help is sought, the worker must be alert to personal biases and evaluate with the couple attitudes on self-identity versus tasks, what it means to have chosen a partner of the same sex, and the desire to be creative versus fears of failure or stereotyping by others. Also, the gay couple is frequently unsettled while they chart

nontraditional paths and may need help in understanding that task assign-
ments based on new interests or the discovery of new abilities can be
changed in the future. In any event, support of strengths within each
person and within the couple as a unit is essential.

Fred, who had a master's degree in English, has had a three-year
relationship with Vic, a trucker. The two had met in a bar when Fred was
a graduate assistant. Both had shared an interest in disco music and danc-
ing, going to museums, gardening, and making a home together. Vic
appreciated Fred's intellectualism and gourmet cooking. When Fred had
difficulty finding a job, though, tension became severe. Fred felt that
Vic was "keeping him" and that by spending his time between job interviews doing the cleaning, cooking, and gardening, he had assumed a sub-
ordinate "housewife" position. Meanwhile, Vic felt that Fred had begun
to deprecate him for his lack of formal education, grammatical errors,
and inability to discuss poets. Problems were further compounded by
Fred's friendships with three gay men he had known in college. "What's
he doing with other guys all the time I'm on the road?" Vic continually
wondered. This problem involved the self-esteem of each client and trust.
The self-esteem difficulties stemmed from matters of status—educational
and occupational; financial contributions versus task contributions; and
role definitions. Difficulties related to trust were revealed in their sexual
life and in their attitudes toward old friends.

Even if the couple has resolved issues related to time, money,
space, and roles, problems may arise over existing significant others.
Visits to and from the "in-laws" may be stressful. Tension is generally
related to the degree to which each member has come out to self and to
others both as an individual and as part of a couple. Furthermore, the
degree to which members of the families accept the gay relationship is
highly significant. Each partner may need to decide whether to risk loss
of family acceptance through overt acts of affection or to suppress any
indications that the relationship is more than a good friendship. Setting
up pseudo-separate bedrooms or rehearsed behaviors to conceal the relationship frequently requires ever more duplicity. Problems in communication often arise. Helping should attempt to identify the factors necessary
for self-esteem. Each partner must then assess what is essential for the
couple's living arrangement to be comfortable and review where their
needs are complementary and where compromise is possible.

Problems with families frequently occur because the homophobia of one or both breaks down coping mechanisms in dealing with the felt threats of the gay relationship. However, if the families can deny the full implications of the relationships, harmony can be maintained. That is, family members can accept a caring relationship if they do not have to deal with its sexual implications. As one young woman phrased it, "My parents just don't hear what they don't want to," and numerous gays have stated variations of that theme. When this denial is occurring, the counselor must help the gay couple understand that to break down such coping processes would be destructive. Parents are not omniscient or totally ready for disclosure.

Family members sometimes defend themselves from their own relative's gayness by projecting responsibility or blame onto the partner. Feelings of being pulled in all directions, love for family and for mate, or anger that one's partner is being hurt by others may obscure the hurt to self-esteem. It may even become easier to accept others' negative evaluations of the partner than to confront the family. The worker's task here is to explore how important the family members are. In other instances, blame and projected guilt from relatives can cause anxiety about the need to declare one's independence from the family. Confronting the fact that deprecation of one's partner is a negation of one's own identity and dealing with fears of loss of family become critical for the couple. The crisis may be heightened when compared with the degree to which a gay identity is an integral part of self, personal resources, and the strength of the gay relationship. The worker should help each member to answer such questions as: "If I give up emotional or actual dependence on family, can I depend on me?" "Can or should I depend on my partner?" "Can I depend on us?"

In examining responses to these questions, problems for solution can be identified and dealt with. These would include dealing with the capacity of each partner for independence and mutual dependence and preventing the replacement of old dependencies with a new, smothering relationship.

Problems related to space, time, and money can be exacerbated if any or all of these resources must be shared with relatives. Having family members move in either temporarily or permanently creates a need for problem solving, especially if there has not been tacit or overt acceptance of the couple's relationship as a viable unit. However, even brief time with the families requires meaningful communication about its implications for the gay relationship. How will traditional holidays be managed?

Where will vacations be spent? How much time visiting relatives is reasonable? How much money is reasonable for gifts for a family member (especially if incomes vary or if one family is large and the other is small)? What if one family accepts the gay relationship but the other does not? If these issues cannot be resolved within a framework of cooperative communication, the ensuing resentments can create severe problems. The worker must return to issues related to trust and values, which create conflicts needing clarification of values. Only with such understanding can the couple examine compromises and generalize from the resolution of one problem to problem solving in the future.

Resentments can also occur over friendships. Old friends and, more importantly, former lovers must be integrated into the friendship network of the couple. The degree of trust each individual has in self, partner, relevant others, and the relationship affects the inclusion of friends. The primary nature of the sexual, affectional, and social affiliation of the partners must be communicated to the friends. Other friendships can then be differentiated in terms of emotional investment and concerns. Jealousy usually reflects lack of trust, but among gay couples it also relates to false beliefs in the instability of homosexual relations and the predatory, sexualized behavior of gays. It may be true that some friends are constantly "on the make." Therefore, open communication among all individuals about acceptable roles and behaviors under the present circumstances is essential. Although the time invested in friends may be presented as the primary problem in the relationship, even more important is the degree to which the client's self-esteem grows from the partner's attention to and from old friends. Jealousy becomes expressed primarily in terms of "you" and "them" with little recognition of what the "I" is bringing to the situation. If the individual cannot recognize any ways in which self-worth is enhanced by the partner's involvement with others, then the couple needs to examine their behaviors and interactions. The goal is not to recall painful events but to determine what would alleviate the negative feelings being experienced and to strengthen those responses that add to the relationship.

Generally, a couple's common interests reflect prior experiences with others. Including those others provides input into the couple as a system and can improve the quality of their interactions, expecially if the couple is not frightened of age differences, nongays, or opposite-sex friendships. While any person prefers certain relationships for certain activities, it also is true that persistent social homogeneity is likely to stultify a relationship. The counselor's role of assessing strengths and assets as well as fears and stereotypes adds an extra dimension that is not encountered in working with nongays.

In moving from the romantic phase to the routine of daily living, problems most often arise because of defensiveness or the absence of communication in the social, economic, and affectional areas that influence survival, security, and self-esteem as a gay couple in a heterosexist world. Although an individual may have resolved problems in establishing a gay identity or never encountered any, the social ramifications for the couple may cause inner conflict or arouse previous conflicts. If one partner is in pain, the other will feel badly. Help for the couple together is usually preferred, but the counselor must be open to seeing only one partner if the other cannot come. Too many gay clients have reported trying to get help from particular agencies in which either the counselor refused to consider the couple as partners or in which policy demanded that both persons come in. Obviously, with such rigid requirements some clients are not going to be helped.

The focus in either joint or individual interviews will, of course, begin with the particular presenting problem. However, the counselor must be alert to the need of the couple to develop and use various resources that can support the relationship. In a generally hostile world, the gay couple can easily become isolated out of fear of that hostility. In reality, both partners can grow from shared interaction, finding positive supports, and developing ways of dealing with nonsupportive systems together. Reality testing requires communication and implies that each partner has the goal of continued growth separately and together. Since reality includes dealing with homophobic employment situations, the couple may need help in coping with the problems that arise when one partner wishes to be militant but the other cannot. The counselor should be sensitive to the need for healthy paranoia but should avoid being too cautious in avoiding any confrontations or exposure. Crises concerning other people, although hazardous to the relationship, can be opportunities for growth.

Finally, the counselor should be alert to the groups that may be available to gay couples. If the counselor is not aware of any resources, he or she should seek them out or help to develop supportive systems. Realistically, some communities may be so small that they have few other gay couples. The counselor should then help the gay couple relate to nongays who will accept them or relocate closer to a larger city. Moving can be traumatic, but if supportive resources in the new city can be identified before the move, the counselor can soften the impact. However, moving to a new city must be assessed relative to several issues—strengths currently within the relationship, running away from versus seeking increased interactions, and goals for the future, individually and collectively. In the crisis of relocating the counselor should enhance the clients' communication skills. The couple may be focused on particular issues and oppressive situations affecting the relationship. However, in counseling, the therapist will ultimately return again and again to what is being said, what is felt but unsaid, what is necessary to improve the relationship, and what is necessary for growth. When the relationship cannot contribute to self- and other-actualization, problem solving then moves into effecting a separation that can foster growth.

Problems with Family Relationships

Most professional literature on child development assumes that the child is in a household with a mother and father. Also, most of the writings and resources for helping single parents assume that the parent is heterosexual. However, an increasing number of gay parents are retaining custody of their children, and some gays are interested in adoption either as a single parent or as a gay couple. These individuals frequently become involved with helping professionals, either because of court referrals or because they are seeking expertise so that they can be effective parents.

In the experience of the authors, many gay parents have resolved identity issues and have significant emotional, social, and economic resources but seek help because of specific concerns about parent-child relationships. Too often, helping professionals have been reluctant to be involved in such cases because of a theoretical bias founded on Freudian or neo-Freudian training or because of their own heterosexism. In actuality, there is no evidence that children raised by gay parents have more problems than children raised by nongay parents or that the children of gays demonstrate inordinate concern about their parents' identity (Woodman, 1979). Important questions in these situations are the following: "When, what, and how do I tell the children about my gay identity?" "If my parent is gay, does that mean I'll grow up gay?" Other issues are how to include a gay partner in the family unit; how to deal with the re-actions of the nongay parent, neighbors, school personnel, and other social systems; and what should be the nature of interaction with other gays and other gay families.

While there is no pat formula for any of the above issues, some dynamics and response patterns can be explored with gay parents and their children. Also, the helping professional has some resources that he or she can use or help to develop for the gay parent and family. Regardless of the problem, the counselor should make sure that each of the above areas has been dealt with, and he or she should be prepared to offer further help in dealing with unresolved questions and issues.

Frequently the parent is sensitive enough to divulge his or her gayness to the child at the appropriate time. If the parent does not do so, someone else may inform the child in a negative or hostile manner and create a crisis. In order to avoid this, counselors should anticipate ques-tions on this subject even when the parent has sought help on another issue. All parents should have regular as well as necessary communication times with their children and engage in active listening; this is an integral part of parent counseling (Janzen and Beck, 1974). The gay parent must also be sensitive to exploring additional questions such as, "Why doesn't Daddy live with us?" "Why do you and Tom live together?" "Are you and Kay both my mothers?" Meanwhile, for the nongay parent, the query "Why doesn't Mommy (or Daddy) live with us?" is more complex than the divorce issue.

What is told to the child depends on the child's age and ability to understand. Even children three, four, or five years old comprehend the meaning of two people loving one another and wanting to care for the child together. Gay parents sometimes rationalize "My parents never discussed what went on in their bedroom with us, so why should I bring this up with my kids?" The counselor must help the parent to differentiate between sharing the caring dimensions of sexual identity and sharing sexual behavior. A first step in this aspect of parental counseling can be to explore how the client's parents expressed affection and the degree to which the gay parent wishes that they did, the ways in which child care was evidenced, and ways in which the client's own parents communicated that love between adults was a good thing that did not diminish the special love for a child. This can facilitate developing ways for the client to share information with the child.

Older children may wonder whether gayness is hereditary or contagious. The parent must understand the need to be objective and informative and to share self-comfort about being gay. However, the counselor may have to help the parent work through negative stereotypes or anxieties about self-identity. The counselor should also reassure the children that they have the freedom to be what is comfortable for them, pointing out that while the parent chose a gay life-style, he or she doesn't think that it is bad, and that he or she obviously did not inherit this particular way of living.

Frequently, a parent underestimates the ability of the child to comprehend and accept his or her gayness. Because of his or her own fears, the parent magnifies the horror of discovery only to find that he or she has postponed opportunities for a closer relationship with the child, increased the child's insecurity about the meaning of honesty and love within the home, or communicated feelings of homophobia that are later reflected onto the parent. When such situations occur, joint parent-child interviews may be helpful. The gay parent should recognize that coming out has obviously been a painful growth process and that some of this pain is now being shared by the child. Dealing with myths and realities openly can facilitate a closer correspondence between parental behavior and words.

In any helping process involving parent and child, any partner of the parent must be included. It may be that the child, who had been living with a gay single parent and receiving undivided attention and love, must now share these feelings with another person. The conflicts that occur when a stepparent suddenly appears can surface along with negative feelings about the homosexual nature of the relationship. The counselor must be attuned to stereotypes that members of the family may have about sex roles and "typical" interactional patterns and to the possibility that family dysfunctioning is blamed on the stepparent or on gayness itself. If underlying attitudes about a gay relationship can be viewed positively, then it will be possible to develop ways for the family members to care about one another and identify ways so that all can grow.

A frequent complication in sharing one's gayness with children is the attitude of heterosexual spouses and the judicial system. Many gay parents are recognized by the courts and former spouses as being the more competent parents as long as the gay identity is not revealed. Children, too, recognize that they are where they truly belong. Although the parent may encourage honesty and openness about the gay identity within the home, the child may have to be told that some things cannot be discussed with other people because it upsets them. Comparisons can be drawn to social taboos such as sexual knowledge, family income, or people's ages. Children are quite sensitive to the reactions of others and to behaviors that might upset their own comfort. Also, the helping professional can assist in this process by conveying the difference between private family business and general information to both the gay parents and the child.

In cases involving custody, it is imperative that professionals objectively assess the capability of parents to provide a nurturing environment for the children, regardless of their sexual orientations. The ability to be flexible, loving, responsible, and open to others does not depend on affectional preference. Also, it is important to assess the degree to which the child feels that these qualities have been communicated. The extent to which members of the social service and mental health professions can determine what is important in child raising will affect court decisions. Therefore, the authors stress once more how important it is that helping professionals eliminate any homophobic attitudes that they may hold.

If the heterosexual parent is aware that the child is living in a household with gay parents, intervention may become necessary to prevent the child from becoming involved in a tug-of-war between the natural parents. Including the nongay parent in family counseling can be very helpful. Roles and rules for interactions among the gay couple, the heterosexual parent, and the child can be set up. The nongay parent may need to understand that the child's self-view reflects in part the views that parents have of each other. If the gay parent is constantly maligned, the child's fears of being gay may be compounded. Exploring the nongay parent's negative stereotypes may reawaken feelings of low self-esteem or resentment toward the gay parent. In such an event, the counselor may be able to initiate individual sessions with the heterosexual parent to minimize friction between the parents and to maximize interaction with the child. The initial focus will be to help the parent deal with homophobia and attitudes toward the former spouse so that they will not interfere with the child's relationships with both natural parents.

The same precepts about private and public information obviously apply to neighbors, playmates, and teachers. The counselor may encounter crises in which acquaintances begin name-calling and insulting the parents and child. In such instances, the therapist's own role modeling is important in showing the child that not all adults and children are bigoted. Generalization about the dynamics of oppression in terms that the child can understand can be valuable. For example, most children have heard peers or adults negatively label others who are different. Parents and child will have to be seen together to discuss how they as a family want to deal with oppressive systems and ways in which the child can find rewarding social contacts that are not threatening. For example, after Ellie was reinforced about the security within her home, she was well aware of the loving and also the differentness of the relationship of her mother and Angie. One day the little seven-year-old commented on name-calling by older neighbor kids, "Gee, it's sad. There are all these people all over wanting to be loved and they yell at you and Angie just because you love each other and me." The two gay parents in this situation had built friendships with other adults based on interests shared by the children or on work associations. In this case, the counselor also responded to the presenting request by the parents—how to locate a nearby Dykes and Tykes group. Counselors can help to start up groups for gay parents without partners when no such organizations exist in their communities.

Some gay parents may state that there were no problems until their children reached adolescence and then began to chastise them because of their gay life-style. The counselor must prevent a rift that could arise because of the parent's defensiveness; the counselor should not begin by stating the obvious issue that problems don't pop up overnight! Educative counseling may be sufficient to weather the storm. Some points to make about adolescents are that they are generally upset by any parental behavior that is "unusual" and that sexuality and sexual identity are big adolescent concerns, which may be exacerbated because of reawakened questions about the relationship between the parent's and adolescent's identity. Understanding the youth's need to establish a separate, individualized identity must be examined with gay parents and child and should include exploration of individual and family goals. The teenager may also wonder about how to deal with peers. Counseling might then include role playing aimed at explaining the family situation to close friends.

Throughout a child's development, gay parents should have recognized the child's reality perceptions and social needs without falling into martyr roles. Gay parents usually need expanded gay social relationships to provide support and validation for their identity and life-style. If parent-child conflicts arise, the following issues should be investigated:

whether the parents have had meaningful peer contacts, whether the child feels excluded or rejected because of the parents' emphasis on the social or political gay world, and to what extent social contacts have been responsible role models for the child. During breakup, if a child has been part of the family, he or she must be included in pre- and postseparation counseling. This also applies to the initiation of relationships. The child in such counseling will need support from all involved to feel continued family security. Including the child in counseling at this time may prevent the gay parent from blaming the termination of the relationship on the child.

The basic purposes of parent-child counseling, including gay and natural parents, are to support open communication, responsible parent-child behavior, continuity of positive family relationships and other support systems, and the alleviation of negative or oppressive influences on the family unit. Additional ideas concerning communication are well presented in Berzon's essay in *Our Right to Love* (Vida, 1978). Helping professionals must be aware of their biases and be able to recognize and support the strengths that usually exist between gay parents and their children.

Problems due to Separation

Professional literature as well as song informs us that "breaking up is hard to do." However, for gay partners the process is likely to be even harder because of the lack of traditional supports and institutions. Rarely does the gay couple use legal counseling or have mental health professionals make referrals to attorneys when the couple is concerned with financial and life planning (Bernstein, 1977). Records of financial investments may not be considered as necessary in gay relationships as they are for a legally married couple, who must consider whether to file a joint income tax, records for insurance purposes, and so forth. Fear of rejection by an arbitrator can prolong debate between a separating couple or increase anger and resentment. Therefore, the counselor's use of appropriate legal resources can be an important part of problem solving. Although some of the pragmatic issues can be effectively handled by interdisciplinary counseling with both gay partners, the mental health counselor must be alert to displacement of feelings of being emotionally cheated onto feelings of being financially hurt. Money and material items can become a means of retaliation for grievances. As in any crisis inter-

vention, separating the issues is essential in resolving the immediate problem. The therapist should structure the interviews to deal with current
issues, alternative plans, and the pros and cons of possible decisions.
Although ventilation can be therapeutic, belaboring the past does not
facilitate growth or resolve problems.

In dealing with emotions, it is not unusual for either or both partners to protest that they should have known that breaking up would
happen or that they had been so sure that this time it would be different.
What clients may be saying is that gay relationships are *always* unstable,
and they may see the present problem as a forerunner of all future relationships. Loss and the blow to self-esteem that usually accompany
heterosexual divorces are present, exacerbated by feelings of the inevita-
bility of breakups, and such despair must be worked through and put in
perspective. Subsequent individual interviews with partners should then
focus on working through feelings of grief, rebuilding self-esteem, and
reassessing myths about gay relationships. Dealing with the loss of a gay
relationship resembles postdivorce counseling. The counselor must be prepared to help the client ventilate anger and hurt, assess what was positive
in this and prior relationships, assess strengths, and teach patterns of interaction for future relationships.

Hopelessness about any committed relationship in the future may
be particularly acute for middle-aged persons, who have added concerns
about youthfulness. As in contemporary Western culture, the gay world
often defines attractiveness to be the latest model's image, which is rarely
over thirty-five. Attention to the latest fads is a part of this, and older
persons may not have the necessary energy for late hours at the "in"
gay bar. Added to this are the possibilities of being cut off from previous
friendships because of people taking sides and the fact that few therapeutic groups exist for gays in need of postseparation counseling. The
resultant feelings of isolation and alienation must be countered by an
assessment of available resources. A first step here would be to examine
the degree to which clients have come out to others, including other gays.
If they have isolated themselves in their relationships and assumed a
pseudo-heterosexual life-style, the pain of the current crisis can be an
opportunity for growth.

Many gay persons have described to the authors the intense isolation and suicidal feelings that accompanied the end of a committed,
closeted relationship. For example, Gloria, age thirty-two, went into a
hospital emergency ward after spending three hours on the hot line telling

the counselor about how she had taken an overdose of barbiturates along with a bourbon and ginger ale. She refused to say why she did this but was persuaded to come in to talk with someone. During the interview, she stated that her gay relationship of eight years had ended three weeks earlier and that she had become increasingly depressed. She contrasted her situation with that of Cora, one of her coworkers. "When Cora's husband left her, she got lots of commiseration from everyone in her family. How can my family understand why I'm so upset because a friend moved out? Cora got time off to see a lawyer to avoid being shafted on money and all the other personnel understood why she sometimes broke down and cried on the job. Who do I go to and who'd care about my eight-year relationship ending? There really was nothing and no one for me any more." After dealing with the anger, depression, and isolation, the therapist may be able to help the client to come out to others.

If the client has come out to others, the counselor can focus on prior and current relationships. The crisis may provide the impetus for examining personal and interpersonal goals, ways of relating to others to attain those goals, and the use of counseling to make desired behavioral changes. The client should be helped to establish contacts with new and old friends and with supportive relatives, which can enable the client to overcome feelings of isolation. The therapist should be aware that gays meet more possible mates through friends than in bars (Bell and Weinberg, 1978; Woodman, 1979).

Finally, the gay client can begin to evaluate committed relationships. Using some of the "if only we had" statements made during the breakup to test what will work in a new relationship can be helpful. Assessing what was positive in the past is also essential, as is identifying the client's own strengths. Identifying the total meaning of gayness and gay identity in gay and heterosexual relationships can also facilitate decision making. The client may very well choose to remain single. Counselors should respect this choice as a means for self-actualization and not become trapped in the heterosexist emphasis on living in couples. What is important is that the termination of the crisis be followed by renewed growth and an increase in available support systems.

Problems of Later Life

"As gay men reach early middle age, they are like their heterosexual counterparts in some ways, and both better and less well 'adjusted' than non-gay males in other ways. The implications for clinicians and others who may deal with homosexual men of middle and later years revolve around the essential normalcy of this group'' (Laner, 1978). A lesbian group organized for older women (Vida, 1978) has made similar findings about women, debunking the myth of the isolated, lonely, or youth-chasing aged gay person. As in other stages of life, the problems for which the elderly gay person seeks help are similar to yet different from those of heterosexual peers. The similar problems involve physical handicaps, loss of the intimate partner, economic hardship, mandated retirement, or the agism of society. Although the counselor will attend to all related physiological and psychological factors in dealing with these problems, he or she must also consider social factors. The elderly person should not be considered asexual.

The responsibility of helping professionals toward elderly gays begins before the clients reach sixty-five. All significant others should be included in preretirement programs, including partners and spouses of heterosexual retirees and lovers of gay retirees. Family service and mental health agencies should also address legal issues in the life planning for gays (Bernstein, 1977). Additionally, middle-aged gay couples are concerned that illness or increasing debility will force them into custodial care where they will not be treated as heterosexual couples are. That is, they will not be allowed to be given necessary medical information about one another, or be able to share living quarters, interact affectionately, or tend to one another's needs.

When gerontological crises do arise, the counselor should listen carefully and assist the older person in identifying who significant others are. The client may have remained closeted to nongays and not tell of any intimacy with his or her roommate. Placement in nursing homes may occur without the counselor having explored the degree to which a friend should feel responsible and want to assume home care. However, if custodial care for one partner should be imperative, helping professionals should consult nursing home staffs to insure that any gay lover and friends would be accepted and allowed to visit.

Another important factor in improving the status of the elderly gay is to initiate or maintain self-esteem and to counterbalance the loss of important relationships. Sharing wisdom is considered significant in mastering this final stage of development (Erikson, 1968). However, few pro-lesbian group organized for older women (Vida, 1978) have made similar elderly gays. For example, in previous chapters, the authors have addressed the need for role models for youth and adults in the process of coming out. Helping professionals could provide the bridge by which people from different age groups could enhance the self-esteem of one another. That such a process is possible has been demonstrated by SAGE—*S*eniors *A*ctive in the *G*ay *E*nvironment, an active group in New York. The potential for engaging elderly gays in such activities is as great as their talents.

Throughout the adulthood of clients, helping professionals must identify and reinforce use of support systems by the gay client and significant others. These supports include intimate others, the family of origin, gay and nongay friends, and medical and legal resources. Political activism by the counselor to oppose homophobic individuals and institutions is as much a part of treatment as is psychotherapy. Finally, if needed supports are lacking, the helping professions must become innovative creators, as we shall discuss in the next chapter.

8

Building Community-Based Support Systems

This chapter discusses social advocacy. It identifies problem areas and reasons for professionals to become involved in resource building, clarifies interventive roles, and lists and describes resources. The authors have stressed that gayness is a social identity that requires appropriate supportive environments for validation. Professionals frequently presume that adequate support systems can either be found or developed independently by gay clients. Usually, however, needed resources either do not exist or can be found only with difficulty. Gay clients often complain of being unable to locate needed supports when they are encouraged to move into a broader social arena. Although identifiable groups may exist in large urban areas, the client who has been relatively isolated or highly mobile may be unaware of where or how to find these.

110

For example, Belinda and her little girl Suzy just moved from Los Angeles to the New York area. Belinda had been very involved with radical lesbian groups on the West Coast but did not know where she could find similar associations in New York. Because Belinda was looking for activist groups that would include Suzy, she felt more angry than isolated by the "exclusive, adults only, speechifying meetings out here" when she could find no groups that would allow Suzy. Suzy was the one who was experiencing loneliness, and her unhappiness precipitated the search for help. Mother and daughter got along quite well, and the counselor's role became one of helping Belinda to meet other mothers so that they could establish a Dykes and Tykes group.

In many communities, small, self-supported gay coalitions are viewed negatively by the general community and are therefore deliberately ignored by such organizations as United Way and social referral services. In other instances, the group members may choose to maintain a low profile so that less open gays will participate. Publicity regarding such associations may be limited to gay publications and mailing lists; therefore they may be unknown to individuals just coming out. In smaller communities gay gatherings of any type tend to remain covert and informal.

Prejudice toward gays in heterosexually oriented groups usually precludes meetings oriented toward gays or the creation of homosexual organizations. An example is the continued absence in many cities of Gay Alcoholics Anonymous groups. Men and women who are willing to acknowledge a problem with alcohol are reluctant to attend meetings in which they cannot relate to heterosexist presentations. However, alternative groups for lesbians and gay men are considered more helpful in the recovery process and are welcomed if they are established. Most people view the support of gay groups or meetings for gays as promoting homosexuality or encouraging the seduction of innocent people. Homophobia and fear of guilt by association in many traditional organizations often dampens the good intentions of the most sympathetic heterosexuals. As a result, gays either abandon their liberal colleagues or work doubly hard to have some impact on the group. Unfortunately, as this impact is felt, many heterosexuals leave the organization, and the vicious circle of rejection and counterrejection continues. This process has been observed by many women in the feminist movement.

For these and related reasons, helping professionals have shown little willingness to redress the negative and isolating social situation of gays. However, if we believe that a gay life-style is a positive and viable alternative, we have the obligation to support and assist gays openly. Support should not be limited to the private acceptance of positive policy statements by professional associations. Although these policies are valuable in establishing a nonoppressive atmosphere for gays, they must be acted on individually and collectively at all social levels.

Professional service must go beyond one-to-one counseling. The first steps can occur within a counselor's own professional setting. If helping professionals really want to help in problem solving with gays, they should profess that willingness clearly and openly to colleagues, board members, and fellow staff. This assertion may provoke the colleagues to reevaluate their attitudes toward gays. In the helping professions, gay caucuses have raised questions about their colleagues' willingness to offer counseling and advocacy services to gays; these questions require program analysis within social agencies. Homophobic attitudes that surface during such discussions must be confronted and resolved.

The following example illustrates some of the problems that may arise. A psychologist in a mental health clinic in a southern city of 100,000 was given the responsibility of forming a unit to serve women in the community. Of the first fifty clients, eight were lesbians with similar presenting problems: isolation, loneliness, and a need to talk with someone. In discussing this with the clinic director, the counselor suggested that the agency initiate a lesbian self-actualization group and publicize it through local public service spots on radio and TV. The eight patients strongly favored a professionally led group that would safeguard confidentiality. As one client phrased it, "Who wants to get clobbered by coming out in a city this size?" The director seized on this example of the town's homophobia and vetoed the idea, saying that there would be too few clients, that the board would not understand homosexuality, and that the lesbians would take over the women's program. The psychologist quoted national statistics indicating that 10 percent of the population is gay and that this percentage probably applied in this city. The psychologist also countered by establishing board-staff in-service training on homosexuality, providing readings for the participants, proving the need for a group, and obtaining support. However, this is a rare success story.

Efforts at reeducation and sensitization should not be limited to those professionals immediately involved in counseling. All personnel in an agency should show the gay clients the same courtesy and respect extended to any other group. When the persons involved in a program have their perspectives in order, it is not sufficient to sit back and wait for the gay clients to arrive. Gays will have little motivation to bring perceived problems to helping settings unless the agencies make clear that they want to help and are willing to accept and respect alternative life-styles. Active outreach to the gay population should be pursued by disseminating information through gay organizations, gay newspapers and newsletters, and gay meeting places. Even with these efforts, building trust to a level where a setting will be accepted will probably be a gradual process. It is particularly important, especially in the early stages of such outreach, to be sensitive to feedback from gay clients concerning the adequacy and appropriateness of the services offered. The clients can offer invaluable assistance in refining service efforts.

Gay caucuses in the local and national counseling organizations are other important means for action and can be a vital source of information concerning related professional issues. These groups welcome more than token support and involvement from heterosexual peers, who can make the groups more effective. Joining a group of peers who are focusing on gay issues requires weighty decision making for the self-identified professional person who has not come out to family, heterosexual friends, or colleagues. However, the complex process of coming out to others carries a high moral imperative in this situation.

The homosexual community in general and gay clients in particular need role models who do not reinforce images of heterosexism and homophobia. Professional schools and departments should make the ethical commitment to reinforce the positive dimensions of a gay identity and to identify counseling issues related to this minority group. Faculties and students can have a far-reaching impact in eliminating myths and stereotypes if they do not perpetuate the image of fear and repression. Learning new attitudes and skills for working with gay clients can begin in the classroom and will enhance the knowledge base of counselors who are already in practice settings. This is particularly true in those areas where the openly gay professional has direct interaction with a variety of colleagues and can continually add to their knowledge.

The gay professional who has come out is also a very important resource for the immediate gay community. Many potential gay clients are unwilling to risk the possible negative reactions from heterosexual counselors. As a result, responsible homosexual professionals can serve as role models for gays who are coming out (particularly young clients), provide security for those who need to see gay counselors, and act as resource consultants for other counselors. Coming out professionally is not easy and may even be prohibited by the work context. For example, a counselor in a high school in a small Utah city indicated that she needed all of her income to support her aging Mormon parents with whom she was living. Although she wanted to come out to others and have her partner join her household, the losses would be more than she could sustain. Meanwhile, she described the pain that she felt at not being able to help the adolescent boys and girls who hinted to her that they were gay but did not know where to turn.

The decision to be open about one's gayness always involves risks, but these can be inflated beyond reality. When losses in relationships are assessed, they often prove minimal when compared with the possibilities to be fully self-actualizing and of greater service. The instance of a psychology faculty member at a large western university demonstrates this point. As a tenured associate professor, Bill had remained relatively closeted and had considered that homosexuality had little relevance in teaching child development or learning theory, his two areas of expertise. He had been oblivious to his colleagues' oppression of gay students until four of them raised the issue tangentially in a class discussion of identity development. Bill then learned that the psychological counseling division of his department refused to see gay students who needed help and had denied use of the facilities for a newly organized gay campus community group. Additionally, no faculty member could be found to sponsor the student organization. After a discussion with his partner, Bill volunteered to become a faculty advisor and confronted his peers with the ethical implications of their homophobic behavior. Rather than encountering any significant negative consequences, he became the gay resource person that his peers had needed.

Regardless of sexual-affectional preference, all helping professionals must confront homophobic attitudes and activities within society. Whether individually or as part of a professional association, we must accept responsibility for our profession's past contributions to heterosexism and homophobia. The opinions of "experts," past and present, are still called upon to reinforce the oppression of gays. The gay community needs the help of professionals who are willing to challenge homophobic assertions and oppressive behaviors. As professionals, we are respected in the community, and our knowledge should be asserted so that homosexuality and the gay life-style can be better understood.

There also are specific areas that generally need attention in most communities. The gay population remains one of the few that is still oppressed by the law. Local ordinances should be enacted through a concerted community effort to guarantee to gays the same civil rights enjoyed by heterosexuals. Professional helpers must also inform the general public. Old prejudices and negative stereotypes about gays neither die easily nor fade away. Appropriate occasions must be chosen to rebut the myths and to present the facts about the viability of alternative life-styles. Opportunities can arise in lectures related to child development, sex education, or family life studies. Almost every meeting at which the professional speaks will have some gay listeners, so presentations should be addressed to gays as well as be about them. The authors frequently have found that a closeted gay person or a concerned relative or friend will seek out the speaker later for private questioning. The presenter may be seen as the first sympathetic individual to whom they can relate their concerns. This contact is vitally important, and the speaker should provide the opportunity for unstructured meeting time. Resource information should also be made available in printed form and given to every member of the audience, because many people who want the information are unable to ask for it.

Informational resources such as libraries should be assessed to see if their materials are accurate, current, and accessible. Many individuals who are in the process of identifying their sexual-affectional preferences turn first to these resources, and this investigation is most likely to occur alone. The ability to remain anonymous is one reason for preferring reading materials to actual discussions. This fact increases the importance that available information be helpful and positively presented. Young persons particularly need to have access to data about the varying expressions of sexuality; therefore, school libraries should also have resources. Sex education efforts should be reviewed to ascertain whether homosexuality is considered objectively and informatively as a nondeviant sexual-affectional preference. Most standard sex education materials in use are less than adequate in this regard. Supplementary materials will often prove necessary, and information regarding additional resources should be provided to all students. This is one way in which the attitudes of society at large can be changed.

In their educational and advocacy efforts, helping professionals are advised to avoid operating independently of the local gay communities whenever possible. We should seek to avoid the mistakes of the past, which included the belief that we could be knowledgeable about gay life-styles from positions as detached observers. Gay networks in any area are very fluid and will be constantly trying different organizational structures, groupings, resources, and leadership. The helping professional will need to be aware of these changes and their significance. Ideally, efforts to educate heterosexuals and to be advocates for homosexuals will take place in conjunction with gays and gay groups. A balanced educational effort should include more than an abstract theoretical perspective. More personalized presentations by those who are willing to share their experiences in being gay are very effective and help to eliminate negative stereotypes.

Another area for professional assistance to the local gay community is the development of adequate support systems for gays. The needs here are extensive and include formal organizations, social networks, and opportunities for interaction in social settings (for example, coffee houses, skating rinks, and bridge clubs). Support systems that help gay persons with problems should be expanded. In large urban areas, the gay community has developed a number of alternative resources such as gay community centers. These systems arose more because traditional helping settings were reluctant to work with gay clients and groups of gays than because of a desire for separatism. As in the example of the lesbian group, the fear of the setting being branded largely explains the lack of development of appropriate services. The fact that gays have developed alternative resources reinforces the inclination to avoid traditional settings. Even when a service is provided, it may be done with considerable ambivalence.

For example, a group of gays involved in peer counseling felt that they went through an annual ritual in finding a location for their weekly sessions. The setting they usually used had a rotating directorship, and with each new director the group's sponsors were invited for a meeting, where they were told that a new location could be found. The reasons, which were never veiled, were clearly related to the old myths and stereotypes. The counselors, educators, and directors who staffed this family-oriented center were convinced that the counseling sessions solely served as opportunities for sexual liaisons. Since the weekly gatherings were carefully structured social growth groups run by a trained helping professional who worked with a broad range of client groups, the difficulties in securing settings where gay persons could meet are evident.

Even if various gay groups are offering services, these resources may be deemed adequate to fill the needs of gays in the area. However, such services and social groups are likely to serve only a small proportion of local gays. Also, many gays will be unwilling, at least in the early stages of coming out to self, to be identified with an openly gay organization. Therefore, traditional agency settings for the closeted gay are extremely important, since the generality of the services offered does not indicate the reason for seeking help. Both the traditional and nontraditional resources are very likely to need continual development, and both types should cooperate closely.

Two approaches for professional assistance might be pursued. The first involves support for settings that gays themselves have established. Many urban areas have small gay community centers serving a broad range of needs. Often these resources are struggling to maintain their existence in the face of limited finances and few trained staff. Although they provide services similar to the nonprofit agencies intended primarily for heterosexual clients, they frequently are unable to obtain traditional sources of funding. The United Fund has shown little understanding or desire to contribute. Therefore, assertive advocacy by helping professionals coupled with information about the efficacy of such gay centers can be invaluable. Another potential source of funding is government grants. However, members of gay organizations may lack the necessary expertise to obtain these funds, so they will need to consult knowledgeable professionals. Volunteer service at gay centers should be undertaken. Like many gays who will not seek help from traditional resources because of their fear of rejection, many professionals seem fearful of being associated with openly gay organizations, perhaps because they fear oppression from their peers. When professionals admit to feeling guilt from association, consideration of homophobia is very much in order. Offering volunteer professional services can be productive for all concerned. The counselor who is relatively unfamiliar with the specific needs of gays and available resources learns a great deal. Also, prospective clients obtain counseling resources that otherwise might not be sought out. If a diversity of helping professionals becomes involved with such centers, they gain credibility among the larger community.

Professionals can also intervene by enlisting gays in their agencies. Gay facilitators in self-actualizing groups can greatly enhance efforts to help other gays deal with and develop their identity. This connection with gays from the community can prove particularly important in small towns or cities where alternative organizations do not exist. Another area where professionals can help is in the provision and supervision of services for gay children and adolescents. Probably no other group in the gay community is so inadequately served, because the myths about "recruiting" young people into a homosexual orientation make it nearly impossible for the adult gay community to reach out to young gays. Until society has learned the value of contact between older and younger gays, heterosexual adults will have to lead social and educational opportunities for young gays.

Assistance in development of nontherapeutic resources will depend on the needs of the local gay community. Establishing informal social networks for gays who cannot be allied with openly gay organizations should be seen as another priority. Social alternatives to gay bars should be available, and will probably be needed to locate meeting places. Fears about the purposes for such gatherings will be allayed when helping professionals support the local gay community's needs.

As resources for gays are developed and identified, some type of directory should help gays locate them. Information and referral agencies should be checked periodically to assure that records are current. Where data is wrong, it should be corrected. A special training session with information and referral workers about how to assist the gay caller may be needed. While preparing this book, the authors contacted an information and referral agency to ask for resources on behalf of a hypothetical adolescent who had come out to self and was seeking gay organizations. After a fifteen-minute wait, the phone worker provided six possibilities. Five of these were strictly for adults, and one of these was the currently nonfunctioning organizing committee for the annual gay community ball!

Gays who call for information may be the most isolated and most conflicted about their sexual-affectional identity. Where possible, establishing a gay hot line is highly desirable. Many troubled gay persons who would not contact general crisis lines use this service where it is available. Recruiting professionals from various disciplines to respond to troubled gays can be another valuable service.

Finally, those counselors who are most willing to be involved can join gays in the public struggle for equal civil rights. Discrimination against gays has been and remains a part of our society. Gay activists who work against oppression need all allies, particularly accredited professionals who can be very effective in community strategies. Again, gay or straight, the professional who avoids such responsibility for fear of becoming too closely identified with gays might well do some soul-searching regarding vestiges of homophobia in self. Certainly, there is much to be done, and many people are needed to improve the personal lives and social environments of gays.

Resources to Be Used or Developed

Because of a lack of financial resources and frequent changes in volunteers and paid personnel, many gay organizations have different addresses and phone numbers from year to year. Also, some communities do not have some important resources. Consequently, we will describe major national organizations and groups that offer social, informational, religious, political, and counseling services for gays in many cities throughout the country. If an area does not have specific support systems, it is the responsibility of helping professionals to form coalitions with one another and with gays to develop them. The addresses of some major headquarters of organizations have been listed so that information can be obtained from them for help in local efforts.

Social and Informational Resources. Many college campuses have registered organizations that serve the needs of gay students and community members. In addition to providing social contacts, they act as a reference point for other resources. For example, many campus groups have listings of sympathetic counselors for gays. The names of college groups may vary, but the national headquarters for approximately 100 such groups is the Gay Academic Union, P.O. Box 927, Los Angeles, Calif. 90028, phone 213-656-0258. Guides to other student resources may be obtained from the National Gay Student Center, 2115 South St., N.W., Washington, D.C. 20008.

Women may find local representatives of the Lesbian Connection, Box 811, Lansing, Mich. 48823. These individuals are part of an international network for gay women who are moving, traveling, or in the process of coming out.

Gay bars and coffee houses usually have information about community groups, meeting times, and publications. Data about such public facilities can usually be obtained most easily from local taxi drivers, but Gaia's Guide, 115 New Montgomery St., San Francisco, Calif. 94105, provides nationwide listings of various local resources.

Feminist bookstores usually post information about current happenings and groups. Even when bookstore proprietors have no direct relationship with lesbians, they usually know about the local scene. Bookstores often stock the publications referred to in the bibliographies, new gay literature, Gaia's Guide, and local gay publications.

Women's centers and feminist counseling agencies frequently post information about lesbian activities and have information about male and female groups. They usually know about local legal, alcoholism, counseling, spiritual, and other resources. The Project on the Status and Education of Women within the Association of American Colleges (1818 R St., N.W., Washington, D.C. 20009) has updated listings of "Women's Centers: Where Are They?" since 1974. Six hundred and fifty centers are included.

Dykes and Tykes can provide a variety of social, legal, and self-actualizing activities for gay parents and their children. Other lesbian groups almost always make provisions for child care during events, but this organization meets more specific needs. The mailing address of the New York chapter is Box 621, Old Chelsea Station, New York, N.Y. 10011. The chapter publishes a bimonthly newsletter, available for $3.00 annually.

The Southern California Women for Understanding was founded in 1976 for lesbian career women who felt a need for a compatible support group. While respecting the confidentiality of members who cannot come out in the work world, the group is working to dispel myths and stereotypes. Other communities are beginning to organize similar professional groups for men and women.

Religious Organizations. Religious organizations provide for spiritual needs and often offer counseling services and social and recreational activities. They are also in the vanguard of advocacy for gays. Adolescents often find social supports through such church groups. Many cities and college campuses have Metropolitan Community Churches, which offer a nondenominational, Christian service for gays. Further information may be obtained from Metropolitan Community Church, Box 1757, New York, N.Y. 10011, phone 212-691-7428; or Box 5770, Los Angeles, Calif. 90055.

Dignity is a resource for Roman Catholics who wish to retain affiliation with their religion. Because many Catholics are reluctant to contact their local parish priest, and since some diocesan centers refuse to provide information, counselors may need to obtain information from Dignity-National, 755 Boylston, Boston, Mass. 02116.

For Episcopalians, there is Integrity, which serves purposes that are comparable to Dignity's. If the diocesan office has no information, contact Integrity/San Francisco, P.O. Box 6444, San Francisco, Calif. 94150, phone 408-268-3378; or Integrity, 701 Orange Street #6, Fort Valley, Ga. 31030.

Helping professionals should seek out spiritual resources and assess attitudes of local religious facilities for clients. Through such exploration, clients can avoid rejection and have meaningful experiences. For example, New York City has a gay synagogue; Washington, D.C., has the Unitarian Gay Community as part of the All Souls Unitarian Church; and Lutherans Concerned for Gay People functions in Los Angeles, Chicago, and some other cities.

Political and Advocacy Resources. The following organizations represent some of the major organizations that have existed for some time and that have nationwide affiliations. For general needs, counselors will be able to identify self-designated local groups through the National Gay Task Force, 80 Fifth Avenue, New York, N.Y. 10011. NGTF maintains up-to-date records and is particularly active in civil rights for gays. A phone call to 212-741-1010 can provide much information on resources helpful to gay clients.

Gay Activist Alliances are concerned with issues of concern to men and women. They may offer classes for newcomers as well as work on public relations and legal issues. The New York City chapter, at 399 Lafayette St., may be of help in organizational efforts.

For lesbians, the Daughters of Bilitis has groups in various parts of the country, but the national headquarters is at 1209 Sutter St., San Francisco, Calif. 94109.

Gay Task Forces and Gay Consciousness Raising Groups are parts of many chapters of the National Organization for Women. Because such activities may be temporary, local chapters must be consulted.

Counseling Resources. Counseling resources may exist under such headings as "Gay (or alternative) counseling services," "gay (lesbian, alternative, or fourth world) resource centers," or "counseling for sexual minorities" in telephone or local community agency directories.

Additional resources can be found through gay caucuses of professional organizations. Among these are the Task Force on the Status of Lesbian and Gay Psychologists, BSERP, American Psychological Association, 1200 17th St., N.W., Washington, D.C. 20036; and the National Association of Social Workers, 1425 H Street, N.W., Suite 600, Washington, D.C. 20005. Local chapters of such organizations should be able to identify reliable community resources.

Finally, there are groups such as the National Association of Lesbian and Gay Gerontologists (3312 Descanso Dr., Los Angeles, Calif. 90026), which includes professionals from all disciplines who are interested in aged gays.

Remembering the caveat about address and phone changes, the reader may also consider the thirty-four-page city by city listing in Vida (1978).

Counselors who are acting on behalf of gay clients must double-check the philosophy, membership, and current activities of any resource before making a referral. Members of various disciplines identify themselves in the Yellow Pages and in gay and feminist publications as therapists for gays, lesbians, or clients concerned with identity issues. However, their theoretical approach may be highly heterosexist. For example, some such counselors believe that no lesbian seen in treatment has ever had a positive relationship with her father and that a goal in treating all gay males is to help them resolve the narcissism that impedes committed relationships. Also, some local community organizations may abandon prior stances or the position of the national organization. For example, they may be so militant or separatist that they are inappropriate for gays who are just in the process of coming out to others. Thus, the professional's verification procedures have at least three functions. First, the client is not placed in jeopardy through an ill-advised referral. Second, the counselor keeps abreast of the current status of the gay community and organizations. Third, organizational and advocacy efforts can be initiated, reinforced, and utilized most appropriately to facilitate self-actualization for gays.

Annotated Bibliography

Abbot, S., and Love, B. *Sappho Was a Right-On Woman.* Briarcliff Manor, N.Y.: Stein & Day, 1973.
Subtitled *A Liberated View of Lesbianism,* this book graphically describes the pragmatic and emotional problems of being closeted. Abbot and Love then discuss the history of feminist and lesbian liberation movements, including some of the problems and the many joys felt by activists.

Atkins, M., and others. "Brief Treatment of Homosexual Patients." *Comprehensive Psychiatry,* 1976, *17* (1), 115-124.
A helpful discussion of the use of crisis intervention in working with gay clients who encounter stress in daily living. The Brief Treatment Service of the Department of Psychiatry, College of Medicine, University of Cincinnati provides for three sessions of intervention intended to help patients who have had a recent crisis to resolve it by rapid treatment. This brief treatment was found to be especially effective with patients who could marshal emotional strengths. What is significant is the authors'

awareness of their own biases in treating gays and their emphasis on viewing "the homosexual patient as a person with a problem, rather than a homosexual problem."

Beaton, S., and Guild, N. "Treatment for Gay Problem Drinkers." *Social Casework,* 1976, *57* (5), 302-308.
This article describes the application of group techniques to working with gays. Establishing an accepting treatment milieu, building trust, and avoiding a "change in orientation" perspective in counseling are emphasized.

Bell, A. P., and Weinberg, M. S. *Homosexualities: A Study of Diversity Among Men and Women.* New York: Simon & Schuster, 1978.
An important sociological study of the diversity in gay and lesbian lifestyles. The authors present the results of extensive research on the San Francisco gay communities and on closeted men and women. Bell and Weinberg acknowledge the limitations of their sample, especially regarding women, but they have included data on ethnic minority gays and the variation in the gay life-style.

Bernstein, B. E. "Legal and Social Interface in Counseling Homosexual Clients." *Social Casework,* 1977, *58* (1), 36-40.
A helpful overview of legal issues relevant to working with gay clients. Because few laws concern gay relationships, a special set of problems arises for some gay people.

Brown, R. M. *A Plain Brown Rapper.* Oakland, Calif.: Diana Press, 1976.
This collection of essays and commentaries presents a radical lesbian-feminist view of women's life-styles, rights, and responsibilities. Rita Mae Brown is an advocate for poor and Third World women and presents strategies to combat oppression. The reader is also referred to Brown's novels for some of the wittiest yet most realistic descriptions of lesbian experiences.

Chafetz, J. S., and others. "A Study of Homosexual Women." *Social Work,* 1974, *19* (6), 714-723.
This article reviews the very limited and biased literature about lesbians. The authors then present data based on fifty-one in-depth interviews and conclude that women are indeed striving toward self-actualization and are entitled to support from helping professionals.

Clark, D. *Loving Someone Gay.* Millbrae, Calif.: Celestial Arts, 1977. This book is an excellent resource for gays who are coming out to self and others. Therapists can also benefit from Clark's examples and analysis of variations in the gay life-style and the counseling process.

Damon, G. "The Least of These: The Minority Whose Screams Haven't Yet Been Heard." In R. Morgan (Ed.), *Sisterhood is Powerful.* New York: Vintage Books, 1970
This lesbian author describes the effects of a male-oriented society on lesbians as a group. The article explains oppressive dynamics resulting from homophobic and sexist social attitudes. It is most helpful in distinguishing between the lesbian and the gay male social situations.

Dank, B. M. "Coming Out in the Gay World." *Psychiatry,* 1971, *34,* 180-195.
This study explores the cognitive processes that are a part of a homosexual identity and how they affect the process of coming out. The authors point out that one of the main functions of the view of homosexuality as a sickness is to inhibit the development of a homosexual identity.

DeMonteflores, C., and Schultz, S. J. "Coming Out: Similarities and Differences for Lesbians and Gay Men." *Journal of Social Issues,* 1978, *34* (3), 59-71.
The authors examine psychological theories related to the process of coming out and identify differences in this process for men and women.

Fairchild, B., and Hayward, N. *Now That You Know: What Every Parent Should Know About Homosexuality.* New York: Harcourt Brace Jovanovich, 1979.
A particularly valuable book authored by two parents of gays. It offers practical insight and advice to parents trying to deal with the trauma experienced when they learn that they have a gay child. The book can also offer considerable insight to gays and helping professionals.

Fink, P. "Homosexuality—Illness or Life-Style?" *Journal of Sex and Marital Therapy,* 1975, *1* (3), 225-231.
This article addresses the issues of labeling, discrimination, and the psychiatric role of treating gays with problems rather than of "assuming the job of society's regulator and judge of acceptable behavior." It contains

a good discussion of the differentiation between gender dysphoria (trans-sexuality) and homosexuality.

Freedman, M. *Homosexuality and Psychological Functioning.* Belmont,
    Calif.: Brooks/Cole, 1971.
Freedman provides an excellent review of concepts and research related
to the issue of psychological health and homosexuals. The conceptual and
therapeutic insights are well integrated.

Goodman, B. *The Lesbian: A Celebration of Difference.* Brooklyn, N.Y.:
    Out and Out Books, 1977.
This book presents a case for advocacy by helping professionals in its
discussion of lesbian motherhood.

Hall, M. "Lesbian Families: Cultural and Clinical Issues." *Social Work,*
    1978, *23* (5), 380-385.
The author explores how knowledge from both a cultural and a clinical
perspective must be a part of helping lesbian couples. This multilevel
approach addresses self-exploration by the worker, clinical tools, and
advocacy on behalf of lesbian clients.

Jay, K., and Young, A. *The Gay Report.* New York: Summit Books, 1979.
A very readable presentation of the results of an extensive questionnaire
responded to by 1,000 lesbians and 4,000 gay men. The book gives a very
detailed and broad picture of homosexual life, and it supports the con-
cept of variations in the gay life-style.

Karr, R. G. "Homosexual Labeling and the Male Role." *Journal of Social
    Issues,* 1978, *34* (3), 73-83.
An experimental study that tries to gauge the perception and behavior of
task groups toward a man who is labeled as a homosexual. The authors
relate the homophobic attitudes of some group members with their
negative impacts on the labeled individual.

Katz, J. *Gay American History.* New York: Crowell, 1976.
This book provides a wealth of historical data related to homosexuality,
discussing everything from the earliest colonial records up to the gay
liberation movement. Katz has included extrapolations from relevant
documents and original material by the author, which makes the book
very readable.

Klein, C. *The Single Parent Experience.* New York: Avon, 1973.
While valuable for its insights regarding the issues related to single parenting, of particular interest is the section "Homosexual Parents." This presents a sensitive and balanced look at both the parent's and children's points of view.

Laner, M. R. "Growing Older Male: Heterosexual and Homosexual." *The Gerontologist,* 1978, *18* (5), 496-501.
A study of responses to personal want ads. The author was concerned with notions regarding the presumed accelerated aging among homosexual men and their supposed preference for younger partners. These notions were not supported by the findings. The article is of value to the geriatric counselor in relating to aging men regardless of sexual orientation.

Masters, W. H., and Johnson, V. E. *Homosexuality in Perspective.* Boston: Little, Brown, 1979.
Despite its heterosexist bias, this study provides information that will help counselors to understand sexual functioning between partners of the same sex. Sex therapists should find the sections dealing with the treatment of homosexual dysfunction of special value.

Miller, I. *Patience and Sarah.* New York: Fawcett Crest, 1969.
This novel, based on historical documents, describes the self-actualization of two women involved in a lesbian relationship during the 1800s. The author's positive approach is counter to the usual negative treatment in many gay novels.

Miller, J. S. "Choosing a Compatible Therapist." *Advocate,* January 26, 1977, pp. 16-19.
Miller advises gay readers about the attitudes of therapists toward gays and about choosing a therapist. The article helps professionals to be sensitive to the concerns of their gay clients.

Norton, J. L. "The Homosexual and Counseling." *Personnel and Guidance Journal,* 1976, *54* (7), 374-377.
This article clarifies terms and offers counseling responses to some of the problems frequently presented by clients. It also presents arguments about the mental health values of coming out to others and emphasizes the need for school counselors to help support systems for gay youth.

Osman, S. "My Stepfather Is a She." *Family Process,* 1972, *11* (2), 209-218.
An instructive case study of a family situation involving a lesbian couple and the fifteen-year-old son of one of the women.

Riddle, D. I., and Sang, B. "Psychotherapy with Lesbians." *Journal of Social Issues,* 1979, *34* (3), 84-100.
This article traces three aspects of women's socialization—self-concept, feminine sex-role behavior, and sexuality—which have particular implications for lesbians. Basing one's self-esteem on others due to women's conditioning is noted. The article also discusses the need in psychotherapy to distinguish between personal problems and social problems relating to the client's lesbian identification. The author also describes therapeutic approaches that avoid heterosexual bias. This is an excellent article that has a long list of references.

Ross, H. L. "Modes of Adjustment of Married Homosexuals." *Social Problems,* 1971, *18* (3), 385-393.
A study of eleven Belgian couples in which the husband is homosexual. The research investigates knowledge by the wife of her husband's homosexual identity, reasons for marriage, sources of conflict, and adoptive measures used.

Spada, J. *The Spada Report: The Newest Survey of Gay Male Sexuality.* New York: New American Library, 1979.
A survey of 1,038 gays who responded to a number of topics related to what it means to be gay. This book is valuable for understanding the gay life-style from the perspective of gays themselves.

Tripp, C. A. *The Homosexual Matrix.* New York: McGraw-Hill, 1975.
A book that investigates the many aspects of homosexuality as it exists within a heterosexual society. The book is particularly valuable in analyzing and responding to the impact that homophobic judgments have upon homosexuals.

Vida, G. (Ed.). *Our Right to Love: A Lesbian Resource Book.* Englewood Cliffs, N.J.: Prentice-Hall, 1978.
A very informative collection of articles by lesbians that discuss all aspects

of living a lesbian life-style. Though dated, the resource section may still prove helpful in forming contacts with the lesbian community.

Warren, C. A. B., and Ponse, B. "The Existential Self in the Gay World." In C.A.B. Warren and S. DeLora (Eds.), *Understanding Sexual Interaction.* Boston: Houghton Mifflin, 1977.
A participant observation and interview study of a covert community of gay men and an overt community of feminist lesbians in southern California. The study investigates interactional dynamics with the larger straight community and focuses on the stigmatizing of gays, stigma management, and the process of alternation.

Weinberg, M. S. "The Male Homosexual: Age-Related Variations in Social and Psychological Characteristics." *Social Problems,* 1970, *17* (2), 527-537.
This study found that although older homosexuals participate less in the gay world and are less active sexually, they are not more lonely or depressed than their nongay peers.

Wirth, S. "Coming Out Close to Home: Principles for Psychotherapy with Families of Lesbians and Gay Men." *Catalyst,* 1978, *1* (3), 6-22.
This article offers a very helpful six-stage model of the experiences of heterosexual family members dealing with the revelation of a gay family member.

Wolfe, S. J., and Stanley, J. P. (Eds.). *The Coming Out Stories.* Watertown, Mass.: Persephone Press, 1980.
While *Counseling with Gay Men and Women* was being prepared for publication, Wolfe and Stanley were collecting poetry and prose describing coming out. Their resultant book is a compilation of autobiographical statements from lesbians of various ages and backgrounds. The selections probe the pains and the joys of self-identifying and address the political issues encountered by gay women. The forty-one vignettes in this book portray a very real part of a difficult developmental process.

References

Abbot, S., and Love, B. *Sappho Was a Right-On Woman: A Liberated View of Lesbianism.* Briarcliff Manor, N.Y.: Stein & Day, 1973.

Adelman, M. R. "A Comparison of Professionally Employed Lesbians and Heterosexual Women on the MMPI." *Archives of Social Behavior,* 1977, *6* (3), 193-201.

Alvarez, W. C. *Homosexuality and Other Forms of Sexual Deviance.* New York: Pyramid Books, 1974.

American Psychiatric Association. *Diagnostic and Statistical Manual of Mental Disorders.* (2nd ed.) Washington, D.C.: American Psychiatric Association, 1968.

APA Task Force on Status of Lesbian and Gay Psychologists. "Attitudes Toward Gay Colleagues: Appendix B." In *Final Report.* Washington, D.C.: American Psychological Association, 1979.

Atkins, M., and others. "Brief Treatment of Homosexual Patients." *Comprehensive Psychiatry,* 1976, *17* (1), 115-124.

Barback, L. G. *For Yourself, the Fulfillment of Female Sexuality.* New York: Doubleday, 1975.

Barker-Benfield, G. J. *The Horrors of the Half Known Life; Male Attitudes Toward Women and Sexuality in 19th Century America.* New York: Harper & Row, 1976.

Beaton, S., and Guild, N. "Treatment for Gay Problem Drinkers." *Social Casework,* 1976, *57* (5), 302-308.

Becker, E. *Revolution in Psychiatry.* New York. Free Press, 1964.

Begelman, D. A. "Homosexuality and the Ethics of Behavioral Intervention." *Journal of Homosexuality,* 1977, *2* (3), 213-219.

Bell, A. P., and Weinberg, M. S. *Homosexualities: A Study of Diversity Among Men and Women.* New York: Simon & Schuster, 1978.

Bem, S. L. "Beyond Androgyny: Some Prescriptions for a Liberated Sexual Identity. "In M. Bloom (Ed.), *Life Span Development.* New York: Macmillan, 1980.

Bernard, J. *Social Problems at Midcentury: Role Status and Stress in Context.* New York: Dryden, 1957.

Bernstein, B. E. "Legal and Social Interface in Counseling Homosexual Clients." *Social Casework,* 1977, *58* (1), 36-40.

Berzon, B., and Leighton, R. (Eds.). *Positively Gay.* Millbrae, Calif.: Celestial Arts, 1979.

Birk, L., and others. "Group Psychotherapy for Homosexual Men by Male-Female Cotherapists." In C. J. Sager and H. S. Kaplan (Eds.), *Progress in Group Therapy.* New York: Brunner/Mazel, 1972.

Blair, R. *Etiology and Treatment Literature on Homosexuality.* New York: National Task Force on Student Personnel Services and Homosexuality, 1972.

Brown, R. M. *A Plain Brown Rapper.* Oakland, Calif.: Diana Press, 1976.

Brown, R. M. *In Her Days.* Plainfield, Vt.: Daughters Inc., 1976.

Brown, R. M. *Rubyfruit Jungle.* New York: Bantam Books, 1978.

Bullough, V. *Homosexuality, Past and Present.* New York: Garland Publishers, 1979.

Cammer, L. *Up from Depression.* New York: Simon & Schuster, 1969.

Chafetz, J. S. *Masculine/Feminine or Human: An Overview of the Sociology of Gender Roles.* Itasca, Ill.: Peacock, 1978.

Chafetz, J. S., and others. "A Study of Homosexual Women." *Social Work,* 1974, *19* (6), 714-723.

Chaplin, J. P. *Dictionary of Psychology.* New York: Dell, 1968.

Clark, D. *Loving Someone Gay.* Millbrae, Calif.: Celestial Arts, 1977.

Clark, D. *Living Gay*. Millbrae, Calif.: Celestial Arts, 1979.

Cooke, N. F. *Satan in Society*. New York: Arno Press, 1974.

Damon, G. "The Least of These: The Minority Whose Screams Haven't Yet Been Heard." In R. Morgan (Ed.), *Sisterhood Is Powerful*. New York: Vintage Books, 1970.

Dank, B. M. "Coming Out in the Gay World." *Psychiatry*, 1971, *34*, 180-195.

Deaux, K. *The Behavior of Women and Men*. Monterey, Calif.: Brooks/ Cole, 1976.

DeMartino, M. F. *Sexual Behavior and Personality Characteristics*. New York: Grove Press, 1976.

DeMonteflores, C., and Schultz, S. J. "Coming Out: Similarities and Differences for Lesbians and Gay Men." *Journal of Social Issues*, 1978, *34*, (3), 59-71.

DeRham, E. *The Love Fraud, Why the Structure of the American Family Is Changing and What Woman Can Do to Make It Work*. New York: C. N. Potter, 1965.

Ellis, H. *On Life and Sex*. New York: Mentor Books, 1957.

Erikson, E. H. *Identity, Youth, and Crisis*. New York: Norton, 1968.

Fairchild, B., and Hayward, N. *Now That You Know: What Every Parent Should Know About Homosexuality*. New York: Harcourt Brace Jovanovich, 1979.

Falk, R. *Women Loving*. New York: Random House, 1975.

Ferguson, K. D., and Finkler, D. C. "An Involvement and Overtness Measure for Lesbians: Its Development and Relation to Anxiety and Social Zeitgeist." *Archives of Sexual Behavior*, 1978, *7* (3), 211-227.

Forfreedom, A. *Sappho of Lesbos*. San Diego, Calif.: Andromeda Press,1973.

Freedman, M. *Homosexuality and Psychological Functioning*. Belmont, Calif.: Brooks/Cole, 1971.

Freedman, M. "Homophobia." *Blueboy*, April 1976a, pp. 24-27.

Freedman, M. "Homosexuals May Be Healthier Than Straights." *Blueboy*, April 1976b, p. 28.

Freund, K. "Should Homosexuality Arouse Therapeutic Concern?" *Journal of Homosexuality*, 1977, *2* (3), 235-240.

Gallegos, J. S., and Harris, O. D. "Toward a Curriculum Model for an Interactionist Approach to Human Behavior in Social Work Education." Paper presented at the annual program meeting, Council on Social Work Education, New Orleans, February 1978.

The Gay Collective. "In America They Call Us Dykes." In Boston Women's Health Book Collective (Ed.), *Our Bodies, Ourselves.* New York: Simon & Schuster, 1973.

Geis, G., and others. "Reported Consequences of Decriminalization of Consensual Adult Homosexuality in Seven American States." *Journal of Homosexuality,* 1976, *1* (4), 419-426.

Gittelson, N. *The Erotic Life of the American Wife, A Survey of Her Sexual Morals.* New York: Delacorte Press, 1972.

Goble, F. G. *The Third Force.* New York: Pocket Books, 1970.

Goffman, E. *Stigma: Notes on the Management of Spoiled Identity.* Englewood Cliffs, N.J.: Prentice-Hall, 1963.

Goldberg, G. *Girls on the City Streets.* New York: Arno Press, 1974.

Gordon, S. *Lonely in America.* New York: Simon & Schuster, 1976.

Gould, L. *Final Analysis.* New York: Avon Books, 1975.

Grace, J. D. "Gay Despair and the Loss of Adolescence." Paper presented at 5th biennial professional symposium of the National Association of Social Workers, San Diego, November 1977.

Haley, J. *Problem-Solving Therapy: New Strategies for Effective Family Therapy.* San Francisco: Jossey-Bass, 1976.

Hall, M. "Lesbian Families: Cultural and Clinical Issues." *Social Work,* 1978, *23* (5), 380-385.

Hall, R. *The Well of Loneliness.* New York: Covici Friede, 1928.

Haller, J. S. *The Physician and Sexuality in Victorian America.* Urbana: University of Illinois Press, 1974.

Hammersmith, S. K., and Weinberg, M. S. "Homosexual Identity: Commitment, Adjustment, and Significant Others." *Sociometry,* 1973, *36* (1), 56-79.

Hays, H. R. *The Dangerous Sex: The Myth of Feminine Evil.* New York: Putnam's, 1964.

Hedblom, J. H. "The Female Homosexual: Social and Attitudinal Dimensions." in J. A. McCaffrey (Ed.), *The Homosexual Dialectic.* Englewood Cliffs, N.J.: Prentice-Hall, 1972.

Heilbrum, C. *Toward a Recognition of Androgyny.* New York: Knopf, 1973.

Hersay, T. *Midwife's Practical Directory.* New York: Arno Press, 1974. (Originally published 1836)

"Homosexuality: Tolerance vs. Approval." *Time,* January 8, 1979, pp. 48-51.

Hooker, E. "The Adjustment of the Male Homosexual." *Journal of Projective Techniques,* 1957, *21,* 18-31.

Hooker, E., and Chance, P. "The Facts That Liberated the Gay Community." *Psychology Today,* 1975, *9* (7), 52-55, 101.

Hopkins, J. H. "The Lesbian Personality." *British Journal of Psychiatry,* 1969, *115,* 1433-1436.

Houghton, W. E. "Love." In *The Victorian Frame of Mind.* New Haven, Conn.: Yale University Press, 1957.

Humphreys, L. *Out of the Closets: The Sociology of Homosexual Liberation.* Englewood Cliffs, N.J.: Prentice-Hall, 1972.

Hunt, M. M. *Sexual Behavior in the 1970s.* Chicago: Playboy Press, 1974.

Janeway, E. *Man's World, Woman's Place: A Study in Social Mythology.* New York: Morrow, 1971.

Janzen, R., and Beck, K. *Training in Parenting Skills: Training Manual Number 1.* Phoenix, Ariz.: Phoenix South Community Mental Health Center, 1974.

Jay, K., and Young, A. *The Gay Report.* New York: Summit Books, 1979.

Jay, K., and Young, A. (Eds.). *Out of the Closets: Voices of Gay Liberation.* New York: Douglas Books, 1972.

Johnston, J. *The Lesbian Nation.* New York: Simon & Schuster, 1973.

Jourard, S. *The Transparent Self.* (Rev. ed.) New York: D. Van Nostrand, 1971.

Kanowitz, L. *Sex Roles in Law and Society: Cases and Materials.* Albuquerque: University of New Mexico Press, 1973.

Katz, J. *Gay American History.* New York: Crowell, 1976.

Kimmel, D. *Adulthood and Aging.* New York: Wiley, 1974.

Kinsey, A. C., and others. *Sexual Behavior in the Human Male.* Philadelphia: Saunders, 1948.

Kinsey, A. C., and others. *Sexual Behavior in the Human Female.* Philadelphia: Saunders, 1953.

Klafs, C. E., and Lyon, M. J. *The Female Athlete: A Coach's Guide to Conditioning and Training.* (2nd ed.) St. Louis: Mosby, 1973.

Klaich, D. *Women Plus Women.* New York: Simon & Schuster, 1974.

Klein, C. "Homosexual Parents." In *The Single Parent Experience.* New York: Avon, 1973.

Koedt, A. "Lesbianism and Feminism." In A. Koedt and others (Eds.), *Radical Feminism.* New York: Quadrangle Books, 1973.

Krafft-Ebing, R. von. *Psychopathia Sexualis*. (F. J. Rebaman, Trans.) New York: Rebaman, 1906.

Kuhn, M. "Mobilizing for Aging." *Prime Time,* May 1976, pp. 5-16.

Laner, M. R. "Growing Older Male: Heterosexual and Homosexual." *The Gerontologist,* 1978, *18* (5), 496-501.

Larrick, N., and Merriam, E. *Male and Female Under 18.* New York: Avon, 1973.

Legman, G. *The Rationale of the Dirty Joke, An Analysis of Sexual Humor.* New York: Grove Press, 1963.

Lenna, H. R., and Rollins, H. M. "A Group Approach to Developing a Proactive Identity for Living a Gay Lifestyle." Paper presented at 12th National Sex Institute of American Association of Sex Educators, Counselors, and Therapists, Washington, D.C., May 1979.

Lewis, S. *Ann Vickers.* New York: Doubleday, 1933.

Lichenstein, G. *A Long Way Baby, Behind-the-Scenes in Women's Pro Tennis.* New York: Morrow, 1974.

McCaffery, J. (Ed.). *The Homosexual Dialectic.* Englewood Cliffs, N.J.: Prentice-Hall, 1972.

McCarthy, M. *The Group.* New York: New American Library, 1972.

McCary, J. *Human Sexuality, Physiology and Psychology, Factors of Sexual Behavior.* Princeton, N.J.: D. Van Nostrand, 1967.

Maccoby, E. *The Development of Sex Differences.* Stanford, Calif.: Stanford University Press, 1966.

March, S. *Gay Liberation.* New York: Pyramid Books, 1974.

Marmor, J. *Sexual Inversion.* New York: Basic Books, 1965.

Martin, D., and Lyon, P. *Lesbian Woman.* San Francisco: New Glide, 1972.

Martin, D., and Lyon, P. "Lesbian Mothers." *Ms.,* 1973, *2* (4), 78-82.

Maslow, A. H. *Toward a Psychology of Being.* (2nd ed.) Princeton, N.J.: D. Van Nostrand, 1968.

Masters, W. H., and Johnson, V. E. *Human Sexual Response.* Boston: Little, Brown, 1966.

Masters, W. H., and Johnson, V. E. *Human Sexual Inadequacy.* Boston: Little, Brown, 1970.

Masters, W. H., and Johnson, V. E. *Homosexuality in Perspective.* Boston: Little, Brown, 1979.

Miller, J. S. "Choosing a Compatible Therapist." *Advocate,* January 26, 1977, pp. 16-19.

Milligan, D. "Homosexuality: Sexual Needs and Social Problems." In R. Bailey and M. Brake (Eds.), *Radical Social Work.* New York: Pantheon, 1975.

Money, J., and Ehrhardt, A. A. *Man and Woman, Boy and Girl: Differentiation and Dimorphism of Gender Identity from Conception to Maturity.* Baltimore: Johns Hopkins University Press, 1973.

Morin, S. F. "Heterosexual Biases in Psychological Research in Lesbian and Male Homosexuality." *American Psychologist,* 1977, *32* (8), 629-637.

Morin, S. F., and Schultz, S. J. "The Gay Movement and the Rights of Children." *Journal of Social Issues,* 1978, *34,* 137-148.

Muncy, R. L. *Sex and Marriage in Utopian Communities, 19th Century America.* Bloomington: Indiana University Press, 1973.

Needham, R. "Casework Intervention with a Homosexual Adolescent." *Social Casework,* 1977, *58* (7), 387-394.

Norton, J. L. "The Homosexual and Counseling." *Personnel and Counseling Journal,* 1976, *54* (7), 374-377.

Oakley, A. *Sex, Gender and Society.* London: Maurice Temple Smith, 1972.

O'Neill, N., and O'Neill, G. *Open Marriage.* New York: Avon, 1973.

Osman, S. "My Stepfather Is a She." *Family Process,* 1972, *11* (2), 209-218.

Papashvily, H. *All the Happy Endings, A Study of the Domestic Novel in America: The Women Who Wrote It and the Women Who Read It in the 19th Century.* New York: Harper & Row, 1956.

Parent, G. *David Meyer Is a Mother.* New York: Bantam, 1977.

Pearson, C., and Pope, K. *Who Am I This Time? Female Portraits in British and American Literature.* New York: McGraw-Hill, 1976.

Perkins, M. W. "On Birth Order Among Lesbians." *Psychological Reports,* 1978, *43,* 814.

Petras, J. W. *Sex: Male-Gender: Masculine.* Sherman Oaks, Calif.: Alfred Publishing, 1975.

Pivar, D. J. *Purity Crusade; Sexual Morality and Social Control 1868-1900.* Contributions in American History, Serial No. 237. Westport, Conn.: Greenwood Press, 1973.

Pleck, J. H. *Men and Masculinity.* Englewood Cliffs, N.J.: Prentice-Hall, 1974.

"Policy on Gay Issues, Resolutions Passed by the 1977 NOW Conference." *NOW Newsletter,* May 1977, p. 31.

Pollack, S., and others. "The Dimensions of Stigma: The Social Situation of the Mentally Ill Person and the Male Homosexual." *Journal of Abnormal Psychology,* 1976, *85* (1), 105-112.

Rapaport, L. "The State of Crisis: Some Theoretical Considerations." *Social Service Review,* 1962, *36* (2), 211-217.

Reich, W. *The Invasion of Compulsory Sex Morality.* New York: Farrar, Straus & Giroux, 1971.

Reich, W. *Sex-Pol: Essays 1929-1934.* (Lee Barendal, Ed.) New York: Random House, 1972.

Reich, W. *The Sexual Revolution: Toward a Self-Governing Character Structure.* New York: Farrar, Straus & Giroux, 1974.

Reik, T. *The Creation of Woman.* New York: Braziller, 1960.

"Removing the Stigma: A Status Report." *APA Monitor,* November 1977, pp. 16, 28.

Riddle, D. I., and Sang, B. "Psychotherapy with Lesbians." *Journal of Social Issues,* 1979, *34* (3), 84-100.

Rosen, D. H. *Lesbianism: A Study of Female Homosexuality.* Springfield, Ill.: Thomas, 1974.

Rosenberg, B. G. *Sex and Identity.* New York: Holt, Rinehart and Winston, 1972.

Ross, H. L. "Modes of Adjustment of Married Homosexuals." *Social Problems,* 1971, *18* (3), 385-393.

Roszak, B., and Roszak, T. (Eds.). *Masculine Feminine: Readings in Sexual Mythology and the Liberation of Women.* New York: Harper & Row, 1970.

Rotter, P. *Bitches and Sad Ladies: An Anthology of Short Fiction by and About Women.* New York: Harper's Magazine Press, 1974.

Ryan, W. *Blaming the Victim.* (Rev. ed.) New York: Vintage Books, 1976.

Schur, E. M. *Labeling Deviant Behavior: Its Sociological Implications.* New York: Harper & Row, 1971.

Sexton, P. *The Feminized Male; Classrooms, White Collars, and the Decline of Manliness.* New York: Random House, 1969.

"Sexuality and Lesbianism." *NOW,* November 1976, p. 2.

Sheehy, G. *Passages: Predictable Crises of Adult Life.* New York: Dutton, 1976.

Shiloh, A. *Studies in Human Sexual Behavior: The American Scene.* Springfield, Ill.: Thomas, 1970.

Simpson, R. *From the Closet to the Courts: The Lesbian Transition.* New York: Viking Press, 1976.

Siporin, M. "Social Treatment: A New-Old Helping Method." *Social Work,* 1970, *15* (3), 13-25.

Skultans, V. *Madness and Morals: Ideas on Insanity in the Nineteenth Century.* London: Routledge & Kegan Paul, 1975.

Sommers, T. *The Not So Helpless Female.* New York: McKay, 1972.

Spada, J. *The Spada Report: The Newest Survey of Gay Male Sexuality.* New York: New American Library, 1979.

Strathern, M. *Women In Between: Female Roles in a Male World.* New York: Seminar Press, 1972.

Szasz, T. S. *The Manufacture of Madness.* New York: Harper & Row, 1970.

Szasz, T. S. "Healing Words for Political Madness." *Advocate,* December 28, 1977, pp. 37-40.

Sze, W. C. *Human Life Cycle.* New York: Aronson, 1975.

Task Force on Homosexuality. *Final Report of the Task Force on Homosexuality.* Chevy Chase, Md.: National Institute of Mental Health, 1969.

Task Force on Homosexuality. "Policy on Gay Issues." *NASW News,* July 1977.

Taylor, G. R. *Sex in History.* New York: Vanguard, 1974.

Teiterbaum, M. *Sex Differences: Social and Biological Perspectives.* New York: Doubleday, 1976.

Thomas, W. I. *Sex and Society: Studies in the Social Psychology of Sex.* New York: Arno, 1974.

Thorne, B., and Henley, N. *Language and Sex, Differences and Dominance.* Rowley, Mass.: Newbury House Publications, 1975.

Tripp, C. A. *The Homosexual Matrix.* New York: McGraw-Hill, 1975.

Trussell, J., and Hatcher, R. A. *Women in Need.* New York: Macmillan, 1972.

Usdin, G., and Hoffling, C. J. *Aging: The Process and the People.* New York: Brunner/Mazel, 1978.

U.S. Bureau of the Census. *Census of the Population 1970.* Vol. 1. Washington, D.C.: U.S. Government Printing Office, 1973.

Vida, G. (Ed.). *Our Right to Love: A Lesbian Resource Book.* Engelwood Cliffs, N.J.: Prentice-Hall, 1978.

Wallerstein, J. S., and Kelly, J. B. "Children and Divorce: A Review." *Social Work,* 1979, *24* (6), 468-475.

Warren, C. A. B., and Ponse, B. "The Existential Self in the Gay World." In C. A. B. Warren and S. DeLora (Eds.), *Understanding Sexual Interaction.* Boston: Houghton Mifflin, 1977.

Weinberg, G. *Society and the Healthy Homosexual.* New York: St. Martin's, 1972.

Weinberg, M. S. "The Male Homosexual: Age-Related Variations in Social and Psychological Characteristics." *Social Problems,* 1970, *17* (2), 527-537.

Weinberg, M. S., and Williams, C. J. *Male Homosexuals.* New York: Penguin Books, 1975.

Weitzman, L. J. *Sex Role Socialization in Picture Books for Preschool Children.* Palo Alto, Calif.: Mayfield Publishing, 1979.

West, U. *Women in a Changing World, Collected Writings by Men and Women Caught Between Complicating Values.* New York: McGraw-Hill, 1975.

Wirth, S. "Coming Out Close to Home: Principles for Psychotherapy with Families of Lesbians and Gay Men." *Catalyst,* 1978, *1* (3), 6-22.

Wolfe, S. J., and Stanley, J. P. (Eds.). *The Coming Out Stories.* Watertown, Mass.: Persephone Press, 1980.

Wolff, C. *Love Between Women.* New York: Harper & Row, 1972.

Woodman, N. J. "The Search for Supports: Counseling with Lesbians Who Have Come Out." Unpublished report, Arizona State University, 1979.

Index

A

Abbot, S., 123, 130
Acceptance: dilemmas of, 57-70; process of, 68-69
Active listening, in depression phase, 41
Adolescents: developmental issues of, 72-78; identity confusion among, 78-84; intervention for, 72-74, 77-78, 79-84; and parents, 80-84; and peers, 84-88; and relationships, 104; sexual experimentation by, 74-75, 79; special problems of, 71-88; and stereotypes, 76, 85-86
Alvarez, W. C., 5, 130
American Civil Liberties Union, 2
American Psychiatric Association, 3, 6, 130
American Psychological Association, 6, 24, 122, 130
Anger, in identity confusion phase, 34-35
Assertiveness training, and self-image, 56

Association of American Colleges, Project on the Status and Education of Women of, 120
Atkins, M., 123, 130

B

Bargaining phase: examples of, 36-37; intervention during, 37-39; in sexual identity, 36-39
Beaton, S., 124, 131
Beck, K., 101, 134
Becker, E., 57, 131
Bell, A. P., 2, 72, 107, 124, 131
Bem, S. L., 95, 131
Bernard, J., 124, 131
Bernstein, B. E., 105, 108, 124, 131
Berzon, B., 105, 131
Brown, R. M., 124, 131
Bryant, A., 8

C

California, Proposition 6 in, 2
Cammer, L., 40, 131